D1569624

Kayaking for Fitness

AN **8-WEEK PROGRAM**
TO GET FIT AND HAVE FUN

BY JODI BIGELOW

Kayaking for Fitness

AN 8-WEEK PROGRAM TO GET FIT AND HAVE FUN

BY **JODI BIGELOW** // PHOTOS BY **JOCK BRADLEY**

THE **HELICONIA PRESS**

PUBLISHED BY

 THE **HELICONIA PRESS**

1576 Beachburg Road
Beachburg, Ontario K0J 1C0 Canada
www.helipress.com

Written by: JODI BIGELOW
Edited by: KATHARINE and REBECCA SANDIFORD
Photography by: JOCK BRADLEY except as noted.
Design and Layout by: BETH KENNEDY

Library and Archives Canada Cataloguing in Publication.

Bigelow, Jodi, 1969–
Kayaking for Fitness: an 8-week program to get fit and have fun
written by Jodi Bigelow; edited by Katharine and Rebecca Sandiford; photography by Jock Bradley

ISBN 978-1-896980-37-9

1. Kayaking. 2. Physical fitness. I. Sandiford, Katharine, 1977–
II. Sandiford, Rebecca, 1973– III. Bradley, Jock, 1961– IV. Title.

GV783.B528 2008   797.122'4   C2007-907379-4

ABOUT SAFETY

Kayaking is an activity with inherent risks, and this book is designed as a general guide, not a substitute for experience. The publisher and the author do not take responsibility for the use of any of the materials or methods described in this book. By following any of the procedures described within, you do so at your own risk.

Contents

About the Author

A competitive adventure athlete for more than 10 years, Jodi Bigelow has become one of Canada's best in these grueling multi-sport endurance events. He owes much of his success to his specialization in paddling, often an adventure athlete's weakest discipline. Although adventure racing is his passion, he uses downriver racing (also known as wildwater) and marathon kayak racing to complement his training. Downriver racing has taken him to several World Championships and he was the 2006 Canadian Champion. In 2007, Jodi completed the Yukon River Quest, a 460 mile (740 km) race down a historic route between Whitehorse and Dawson City in Canada's Yukon Territory. Jodi works as a high school teacher and runs Paddlefit, a personal training and corporate team-building business based in Ottawa, Canada. For more information or for personal coaching tips, see Paddlefit.com

Introduction

ALTHOUGH THEY ARE PERFECT for day trips, expeditions, fishing and birding excursions, and a terrific way to mellow out at the cottage, the kayak is rapidly gaining popularity as a piece of fitness equipment. Wherever there are suitable places to paddle, kayaking can be built into daily and weekly routines for achieving total body health and fitness.

The fact is, we're on the verge of a fitness revolution—and it's not just elite paddlers preparing for a race or expedition. A whole new crowd has switched on to kayaking, seeking out the general fitness benefits that it offers—to lose weight, build strength and muscle tone, increase health and to look and feel good.

What is drawing people to this sport now? Many are plagued with injuries from cycling or running. In looking for other ways to stay fit, they discover that kayaking works the whole body, giving an extra workout to the oft-overlooked abs and shoulders. Because kayaking with proper technique works the entire abdominal area, it also develops essential core strength. The importance of core strength as the foundation of total fitness has received a lot of press in recent years. Strong muscles in your abdominal core give you better posture, slim your waistline, and support you physically in every activity from simple everyday movement to running marathons, which also means fewer injuries.

If you use the right equipment, correct technique and paddle on safe waterways, another appealing thing about kayaking is that it poses little risk of injury or accident while still delivering satisfaction and results. Unlike running, kayaking is low-impact—there is no hard pounding to cause muscle and joint damage. Unlike cycling, there is no chance of high speed crashes and what cyclists call "road rash"—scraped skin with embedded dirt from the road.

Kayaking can be used for fitness at all levels and for all ages, from seniors interested in a low-impact sport to younger elite athletes interested in serious competition. Kayaking races are becoming more popular with many short, long-distance and marathon-style events to choose from. Also, multi-sport adventure races, usually a combination of kayaking, mountain biking, trekking and climbing, are ever-increasing in popularity. For those who already participate in these thrilling events, paddling is often the weakest individual element, so time invested specifically in kayak training can bring about the greatest overall improvement in race results.

Through years of working closely with my clients, I've come up with a program that can be used by anyone. Whether you are a fitness enthusiast looking for a daily workout or someone who wants a more relaxed schedule, you will benefit by following the program outlined in this book.

The first four chapters cover basic equipment, proper paddling technique and safety. Then we dive into fitness and training principles, followed by a detailed 8-week kayak fitness program. You can follow the program like it's the law or you can pick and choose elements from it to accommodate more relaxed goals and schedules. Whatever you are looking for, the ideas and techniques are there to help you improve your fitness and overall conditioning. We'll then look at off-season strength and conditioning exercises, and you'll find suggestions for winter activities that complement kayaking. The last chapter discusses some of the many possibilities that your new kayaking skills and improved fitness will open to you.

In the end, no matter what your reason is for getting into a kayak, every day on the water is better and a little brighter than a day not on the water. My sincerest hope is that you come to enjoy the benefits this book is designed to offer!

CHAPTER 1:

Equipment

Your Body

As with any sport, your body is your first piece of equipment. It is an amazing thing. With proper care, rest and recovery, it will adjust to almost anything we subject it to. With that in mind, take care of yourself and never work yourself to the point of injury or strain. Listen to your body as you go. If an exercise hurts or is even uncomfortable, consider stopping and trying something different. Proper exercise does not involve pain. As a general rule, focus on quality, not quantity.

If you are not currently exercising on a regular basis, it is a good idea to consult your doctor before beginning any of the training exercises outlined in this book.

The Kayak

There are many different types and shapes of kayaks available on the market today, and each one is designed with a specific purpose and paddler in mind. In fact, I have seven different kayaks hanging in my garage, and I still have to call up my parents to borrow their sea kayaks for my yearly Georgian Bay trip! Kayaking is such an important part of my life that it makes sense to have a quiver of boats. However most people will only need one boat, so in this section we'll look at the different options that you have and help you choose the right kayak for you.

Kayaks are typically classified by their function and purpose. For kayak fitness, you will want to choose a boat designed for flat water, not whitewater. Flat water kayaks come in one of three categories: recreational, sea or touring, and racing. Any of these types are suitable for kayak fitness. The descriptions below will help you to decide which one fits best with your particular needs.

BASIC TYPES

Recreational kayaks are designed for day trips and are the most stable kayaks out there—having the beginner or safety-oriented paddler in mind. They range from 10 to 15 feet long.

Sit-on-top kayak

Sit-inside kayak

Sea kayaks are long and narrow—designed to travel quickly in variable conditions.

Racing kayaks are tippy, but they glide through the water effortlessly.

Recreational kayaks are available in two self-explanatory styles—sit-on-top and sit-inside—and both are available as singles or doubles (solo or tandem).

Sea or touring kayaks are all sit-inside kayaks designed to travel quickly in variable conditions, although they do so at the sacrifice of some stability. Sea/touring kayaks are longer than recreational kayaks (between 14 and 19 feet long), and they have smaller cockpits that allow for outfitting features like thigh hooks, which offer the paddler much better boat-control and make rolling a kayak possible. They have built-in flotation created by bulkheads which divide the boat's interior into separate watertight compartments. These compartments are accessed through hatches on the deck. Not only do these compartments offer a relatively dry spot for carrying gear for day or camping trips, but they also provide valuable flotation in

case the boat capsizes. Sea or touring kayaks will also have either a rudder or skeg which is used to help the kayak go straight.

Racing kayaks are designed to go as fast as possible on flat, calm, protected waters only. They are made of the lightest materials and have hull shapes designed for speed, not stability. Although there are fairly stable beginner models available, they are still not generally suitable for new paddlers. Sprint kayaks are the fastest racing kayaks, but there are also multi-sport racing kayaks which deal better with rougher conditions.

PARTS OF THE KAYAK

Although the above-mentioned kayaks vary a great deal, they share many of the same parts. The top of a kayak is referred to as the deck. The bottom is the hull. The front of the boat is called the bow, and the back is the stern. On deck, you'll often find deck lines that make it really easy to grab the boat, and bungee cords that you can use to secure extra equipment like water bottles or sunscreen. You'll also find convenient carrying handles at both the bow and stern.

Some boats have a rudder or skeg to help keep the boat running straight (although neither are essential pieces of equipment). Rudders offer much more control as they swivel from side-to-side and are controlled by foot pedals. Skegs are fixed along the centerline on the bottom of the boat and can be lowered to help the boat go straight in windy conditions. All kayaks have some form of seat and support for the feet, such as foot pedals or foot wells. They should also have some type of lower back support, like a back band or a seat back.

Unique to sit-inside kayaks is the cockpit—the area within the boat where you sit. Around the cockpit you'll find the cockpit rim, otherwise referred to as the coaming. This raised lip allows a sprayskirt to be attached to the boat in order to keep water out.

Construction Materials

Kayaks can be manufactured from a wide variety of materials, but fall within three structural classes: rigid, folding and inflatable.

Rigid kayaks are constructed of plastic, fiberglass, Kevlar, carbon fiber or wood. Rigid boats are what most people picture when they think of a kayak. The most common material used to make kayaks is a durable polyethylene (a type of plastic).

Folding kayaks are collapsible boats made of fabric stretched over either a wood or aluminum frame. Most folding kayaks will fit into a backpack-sized bag when taken apart.

Inflatable kayaks are made from coated fabrics, and like folding kayaks, they pack down into a backpack-sized bag.

Sit-on-top kayaks are great for warm environments.

Sit-inside kayaks keep you drier and protect your legs from sun and wind.

CHOOSING A KAYAK

Buying a kayak is the biggest decision you will have to make in this sport, whether you are new to kayak fitness or a more experienced paddler who wants to upgrade to a faster boat and take your paddling to the next level. Why? Because the boat is the most expensive investment you will make—although if you take good care of it, a boat can last many, many years and give you a great return in terms of pleasure and health. Still, whether you fork out $400 or $6000, any amount of money is too much if you get out on the water and find that the boat is unsuitable for your needs. It is essential that you choose a boat in which you will feel comfortable and safe paddling. With a little research, you can make the right choice and maximize both your athletic development and your overall enjoyment.

Sit-on-top or Sit-inside?

Your first and biggest decision is whether to go for a sit-on-top or a sit-inside kayak. There are pros and cons to both. Sit-on-tops are the most user-friendly. Since you sit right on top of the kayak, your legs are totally free (although you can opt to use thigh straps that allow you to control the kayak more with your legs) and there is no feeling of confinement that some experience a sit-inside. Sit-on-tops are also self-bailing, meaning that water automatically drains out of the seat and foot wells through scupper holes that go right through the kayak. Their inherent stability also makes them very safe and fun to use. In fact, they are so easy to get into that you that you can slip on and off them as the urge takes you. If you do capsize, they don't even require emptying out—just flip them upright and scramble back on board! All these features make sit-on-top kayaks great for more anxious paddlers, for paddling in warm environments, and for paddling in surf zones where flipping is a very real possibility.

Although these are some pretty compelling reasons to choose a sit-on-top kayak, there are also some great reasons to choose a sit-inside kayak. In fact, sit-inside kayaks are generally the best kayaks for fitness purposes because they tend to be faster and their design allows you to use a more ideal paddling technique. Sit-inside kayaks also allow you to stay far drier and protect your lower body from the wind. The option of using a spray deck further increases your defenses against cold and wet conditions. For this reason, sit-inside kayaks are popular in areas where cool air and water temperatures are the norm. People who are looking to extend their paddling season into the cooler months of the year will choose sit-insides too. Another advantage of the sit-inside kayak is that they are available in a wide variety of materials, such as lightweight Kevlar, whereas sit-on-tops are made exclusively from durable but heavy polyethylene. The downside of the sit-inside kayaks is that recovering from a capsize is not a simple process. Because sit-inside kayaks are not self-bailing, capsizing will result in a swamped boat, which can be cumbersome to deal with.

TIP

Another factor to consider is that shorter boats are much easier to handle in transport and weigh considerably less than long ones. This is an important consideration for paddlers who will be routinely hauling boats on their own or loading kayaks up onto high vehicles.

Once you have decided on whether to go for a sit-on-top or sit-inside kayak, there are a few other issues to consider. As a general rule, the longer and narrower a boat is, the faster it will be. However, the wider a boat is, the more stable it will be.

You know yourself and your needs best. Consider how comfortable you are in the water, how quickly you learn new physical skills, and how important speed is for you when choosing a boat. If you're new to paddling and speed is not a particular concern for you, a wider, more stable boat will likely be the best choice—particularly if you're not a strong swimmer (although you will be wearing a life jacket at all times). On the

other hand, the human body is a wonderful thing; your central nervous system can adapt to almost any type of new activity you throw at it, so as long as you're comfortable with and prepared for the fact that you might capsize a few times while getting used to a less stable kayak, maybe you should start with narrower and faster boat. As your skills, stability, strength and fitness levels improve you will likely migrate towards one anyway.

TIP

The ability to use your legs—and yes, you can use your legs in a kayak—will greatly improve your padding efficiency. Leg engagement through the use of foot pedals allows you to fully rotate your torso and gain extra power from larger muscle groups (your core and leg muscles). For this reason, foot pedals that also control a rudder are not the best option when it comes to getting the most power for your strokes because the pedals will move when you press them.

The final decision that needs to be made has to do with the material your kayak is made from. As was already mentioned, most recreational boats are made of roto-molded polyethylene (similar to Tupperware). These "poly" boats are amazingly affordable, incredibly durable and they perform very well while requiring the absolute minimum of maintenance or care. The downside is that they tend to be the heaviest kayaks.

You can also get kayaks made from composite materials like fiberglass, Kevlar or carbon which get their structure from a combination of resin and woven fibers. Composite construction produces beautiful, lightweight parts that are stiff and glossy, but they can be much more expensive. Furthermore, they do not handle impact or tolerate general abuse very well. Composite boats are suited to paddlers who want the highest performance and are willing to take extra care of their equipment. All racing kayaks are made from composite materials.

You can also get recreational and touring kayaks made from a thermoform process. These boats are relatively new to the market and are becoming more and more popular. The material used in the thermoforming process provides a great-looking kayak that falls somewhere between composites and polyethylene with regards to durability, affordability and weight.

Folding kayaks are great if transporting or storing a full-sized kayak is going to be an issue. They also offer the only real option of flying somewhere with your kayak. Of course, the luxury of being able to fold your kayak comes at a price! The lack of rigidity also causes these kayaks to be a little bit slower.

Inflatable kayaks have similar benefits to folding kayaks and are surprisingly durable, but their flexibility makes them very slow and therefore not the best option for a kayak fitness boat.

I'm sure it's clear by now that there isn't a single kayak that will work best for everyone. But for the purpose of getting fit, any of the boats described above will do. In a sense, all you really need is a stable, floating platform and a paddle! However, the boat you choose can be a big factor in how much fun you have in your training. In particular, speed and comfort will make training sessions more enjoyable. Once you've narrowed down your options, I highly recommend taking your time and testing several boats before buying one. Most outdoor stores offer demo sessions for this purpose, so make sure you take the opportunity to try before you buy!

Give a good paddle a try and feel the difference.

Paddles

While it is true that almost any paddle will probably do the trick, there are a lot of great reasons to take the time to choose the right paddle for what you want to do. It will make your time on the water more comfortable, more enjoyable and if speed is a goal, allow you to paddle your fastest.

PARTS OF THE PADDLE

Paddles have three main parts to them. They have a shaft, a power face, and a back face. The power face is the side of the paddle blade that catches water when you take a forward stroke, while the back face, of course, is the other side of the blade. From tip to tip, paddles can vary in length from 190 centimeters to 260 centimeters (rarely measured in inches). Blades also come in a wide range of shapes and sizes.

CONSTRUCTION MATERIALS

Paddles are made from a variety of materials. The most common are plastic, fiberglass, carbon fiber or a combination thereof. Plastic paddles offer a decent blend of performance and affordability—costing typically between $60 and $150. Fiberglass paddles are lighter and stiffer (which offers a more powerful stroke) and cost between $150 and $250. Carbon fiber paddles are the lightest and stiffest paddles—costing $250 to $500. If you can afford it, I can tell you that you'll appreciate the feel of a good quality fiberglass or carbon fiber paddle.

CHOOSING A PADDLE

Although this section should inform you enough to make an educated decision about the type of paddle that you're looking for, it's worth talking to an experienced paddler at an outdoors store to help make your decision.

Blade   Shaft   Drip ring

First of all, it's important to identify that there are two different paddling styles: low angle and high angle. These styles correlate to the angle of the paddle shaft in relation to the surface of the water when you take a stroke.

Low angle is the most common paddling style and is used by the vast majority of recreational paddlers out there. It reflects a relaxed approach to paddling, with a slower cadence (turnover of strokes). Low angle is well-suited for recreational paddling or for longer touring days where the paddler will maintain a low heart rate. Paddles designed for low angle paddling have longer and narrower blades with a dihedral power face. A dihedral power face has a raised center line and two faces that slope away on either side to direct the water around the blade. This makes the paddle easier to pull through the water, but sacrifices power to do so. For low angle paddling you'll also generally choose a longer paddle, between 230 and 240 cm.

ADVANCED TIP

The wing blade is a unique design that catches an extraordinary amount of water and provides your forward stroke with the most power, but it does require a slightly different technique to use than standard blade shapes and is not recommended for beginners. Wing blade paddles are for serious competitors or dedicated amateurs looking for more speed.

Swift Racing

A low angle stroke sees your top hand stay below chin level and is a more relaxed paddling style.

A high angle stroke sees your top hand up at forehead level and is a more aggressive paddling style.

High angle paddling reflects a more aggressive approach to paddling. The strokes require more energy, but they propel the kayak forward more efficiently. Paddles that cater to a high angle style are shorter (between 200 and 220 cm), have shorter and wider blades with a concave power face that catches more water during the forward stroke.

For fitness paddling, you'll want to get yourself a higher angle paddle.

To further narrow down what size of paddle you should choose, you have to consider three more things: the design of your boat, your body size and your strength.

Boat design: The wider your boat is, the longer the paddle has to be to reach the water. Similarly, you will need a longer paddle if you are using a sit-on-top kayak because you are sitting higher and further out of the water.

Body size: The taller you are, the longer your paddle should be. The heavier you are, the larger the blades should be.

Strength: The stronger and more fit you are, the larger the blades that you'll be able to manage.

I have a few paddles, each with different blade sizes for different types of races; large blades for sprint racing, and smaller blades for marathon races.

To Feather or Not to Feather?

The last point to consider is the feather angle. Feather is the amount of twist or offset between the blades of a paddle. If paddle blades are not feathered, it means that their blades are on the same plane and both would lie flat if rested on the floor. Feathered paddles have blades that are turned at an angle to one another. Feathering allows for a slightly more efficient stroke because the blade that is not in the water can slice through the air with its narrow edge instead of the flat side. Some paddlers, especially beginners, find that the additional wrist-turning necessary to use a feathered paddle is uncomfortable and unnatural. There is no "right way" here, just personal preference. As a general rule, it's hard to go wrong using a paddle with blades feathered between 0 and 45 degrees.

TIP

Something else you might see on the water are paddles with bent shafts. The goal of bent shaft paddles is to lessen wrist and muscle fatigue by placing the joints of the hand and wrist in a more natural position when taking a stroke. Because of the added complexity of manufacturing the shaft, these paddles are usually quite costly. There's endless debate on how effective bent shafts really are—try one and decide for yourself!

A paddle with a 90 degree, 45 degree, and 0 degree feather.

Safety Equipment

The safety equipment that you should bring on the water is directly related to the area in which you're paddling. In this book, we're assuming that you're staying in flat water conditions that are sheltered from wind and waves, and that you're staying close enough to shore so that as a last resort you could easily swim to safety and walk home. You need to understand that as soon as you venture into unprotected water, paddle alone, or further from shore than you can comfortably swim, the rules change dramatically. In any of these cases you'll need more safety and rescue equipment along with the training on how to use it. If this interests you, ask your local outdoor store about what sea kayaking safety and rescue courses are offered in your area.

With these limitations understood, here's a list of things I recommend you bring with you every time you hit the water. Depending on where you live, some or all of them may be required by law, so it's a good idea to look into what regulations apply to boating in your area.

PFD (Personal Flotation Device): The PFD is your single most important piece of safety equipment and should always be worn when on the water. A PFD should have a number of cinch straps on the sides and at the waist so that it can be tightened to fit like a pair of shoes—snug but comfortable. If it's not worn properly, or doesn't fit correctly, a PFD can actually impede your ability to swim rather than help. A good fit test that you can do on dry land is to put on the PFD and tighten it as you would to wear it on the water. If you then hook your thumbs under the shoulder straps and haul upward, your PFD should stay in place around your body and not ride up around your ears.

Any PFD that is Coast Guard Approved, fits well, and is comfortable enough so that you won't feel the need to remove it while on the water, is perfectly adequate. However, the best PFDs for kayaking are the ones specifically designed for that

Paddling specific PFDs feature large armholes and convenient features like zippered pockets.

purpose. Kayaking PFDs feature large armholes, and the bulk of their flotation is moved down away from the shoulders and upper chest to allow the fullest range of arm and upper body motion for maximum comfort while paddling. Many PFDs also have convenient features such as zippered pockets for carrying such things as sunscreen, glasses, and snacks. Some models even have pouches for hydration bladders that can be mounted on the back of the PFD.

Rope: Some regulations require there to be a rope with each boat. The most practical rope for kayaking is a tow rope. A tow rope (also referred to as a towline)—as the name implies—is used by one paddler to help pull another paddler along. Towlines can be used to help a tired or hurt paddler make headway. Towlines are worn like a belt around your waist or your PFD, and have a quick release buckle for breaking free, a leash that can either be short (5–10 feet or 2–3 meters) or long (30–45 feet or 10–15 meters), and a carabiner or hook on the end for clipping onto the boat that you're going to tow.

Pumps: Unless you paddle a sit-on-top kayak, you'll need a pump system to empty your boat of water should it become swamped. Hand-held bilge pumps are the most effective and practical and can easily be stowed inside or on top of your kayak.

Whistle: A whistle is one of the best ways to get someone's attention. Get a whistle that doesn't use a pea (which will just rust on you) and then tie it to your PFD in a position that allows you to blow the whistle while you're wearing the life jacket. Use three short and powerful blasts to signal a serious emergency, and a single blast to simply draw attention.

Light: If you plan on traveling at dusk, you'll need to bring some type of light. Headlamps are by far the best because they leave you free to paddle, and they can be easily stored in a dry bag. Remember, the light is not just so you can see, but so that others can see you.

A tow rope can be used to help a tired or hurt paddler.

Accessories

Here are a few other things that will make your workouts more measurable and more enjoyable.

SPORTS WATCH

A good sports watch is convenient for the average fitness kayaker, and essential for more competitive racing kayakers. You don't need to spend a lot of money to find something with the following basic and very useful features:

- Waterproof
- Chronograph timer or stopwatch
- Countdown timer

With a countdown timer, you can use the watch to indicate increments of time. Part of the training program I present later in this book uses six minute intervals, for example. With a good watch, you won't have to think about watching the clock; you can let the scheduled beeps let you know when the interval is over.

If you're interested in racing, see if you can find a watch that lets you track split times. When I'm in a downriver or wildwater race, I use it to tell if I am gaining on the racer who started in front of me whenever I pass distance landmarks.

In addition to the basic features listed above, there are a few more things that you might want to look for in a sports watch if your budget allows.

Although it's not necessary, you might consider getting a watch that also has a global positioning system (GPS) and the ability to calculate speed over distances. I have found it very useful for training, but even non-competitive fitness kayakers can have fun with these features. Not only do you get an accurate reading of your speed but some models can also be set to measure exact distances. For distance-based intervals, you can plot out a series of measured stretches of water, rather than just sticking to sections that you already know the distance for.

You might also consider getting a watch that incorporates a heart rate monitor (HRM). HRMs show you precisely how hard you are working and help you exercise in the best aerobic zones for specific types of training. Many HRMs can be set with customized alarms that will tell you when you are exercising too hard or not hard enough. I use heart rate levels as reference points for the training program in this book, so you may find them very useful. More information about heart rates is included in Chapter 5: *Fitness and Training*.

SPRAY SKIRT

If you're paddling a sit-inside kayak, you can wear a spray skirt, also known as a spray deck. The spray skirt helps keep the cold water out of your boat and allows your body heat to

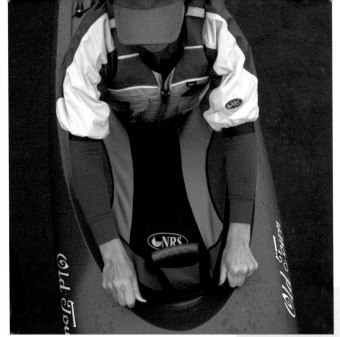

A spray skirt keeps water out of your boat and is a good option in colder conditions.

warm up the interior of the cockpit to some extent. On hot days, the spray skirt will also protect your legs from the sun.

The spray skirt seals off the cockpit of your kayak and keeps water out of your boat while you paddle. It's important to know that spray skirts are not one-size-fits-all. You need to get a skirt specifically sized to your boat's coaming. Spray skirts are usually made out of one of two materials: nylon or neoprene. Nylon decks typically vent better, are easier to get on and to take off, and cost less, but they don't keep as strong a seal as neoprene. Some skirts are hybrids, having a neoprene deck for dryness and a nylon tunnel for ventilation. For the purpose of fitness kayaking, a simple nylon skirt will work well until you take the next big step with your kayaking and start challenging rougher water and learn to roll.

All spray skirts have rip cords that allow you to pop the skirt off the boat when you need to get out.

SEAT PAD

If your kayak doesn't have a comfortable seat, it's worth taking the time to make it so. The easiest way is to start with a mini-cell foam sleeping mat, and then trim and glue it to the seat with contact cement. For my seat, I have created an indented space that my sit bones fit into, which relieves some of the pressure associated with sitting for extended periods.

If you're really keen to get the most from your time on the water, you can then wrap the seat in smooth thick plastic, such as thick garbage bag and then secure it with some strong tape. The plastic top will allow your butt to slide a bit on the seat, helping you get better rotation in your stroke.

SNACKS AND WATER

Even if you don't end up eating it, I'm a huge fan of bringing a snack when paddling. Energy bars are healthy, compact, wrapped in waterproof packaging, and can provide a much-needed calorie boost if you find yourself getting tired or hungry during or right after a workout. Eating appropriate food also helps your body recover faster.

Always keep a water bottle handy and remember to drink from it. You can exercise a well-hydrated body more effectively, and plenty of water is also critical for muscle recovery.

Left: A drysuit is the ultimate defense against the cold.
Right: In hot weather, quick drying shorts and shirt are ideal.

Dressing to Go Kayaking

When deciding what to wear on the water, think about the weather conditions and how cold the water is. No matter what your skill level or experience, you must plan around the possibility of unexpectedly falling into the water. Consider the worst case scenario—the longest you could possibly be in the water and the farthest you'd have to paddle home wet. Reassess these factors day to day and season to season.

WARM WEATHER

Dressing is not a big problem for a hot summer day on warm water. Getting completely wet may be a welcome way to cool-down after—or even during—your paddling session. Your biggest concern on hot, sunny days is staying hydrated, cool and protected from the sun. On these days, I consider a hat, sunglasses and waterproof sunscreen mandatory. For your shirt and shorts, synthetic fabrics that are quick-drying are ideal. Outdoor and paddling stores have an abundant selection to choose from.

COLD WEATHER

Dressing for cold weather on cold water is also straightforward. As with any cold weather activity, layering is the key to staying comfortable. As a base layer, wear a synthetic, form-fitting shirt that is quick-drying and will wick moisture from your skin. This might be the same piece of clothing that you wear as a single layer in warm conditions. Then, depending on how cold the conditions are, add subsequent synthetic insulating layers such as polypropylene, Capilene, or fleece. Over top, you'll want a good waterproof breathable jacket or paddling top to keep wind and water at bay. For your feet, neoprene booties and a pair of wool socks will keep your toes warm. Assuming you're using a sit-inside kayak, a spray skirt also helps trap body heat inside the boat and keeps cold water from splashing into your lap. If it's so chilly out that your hands are getting cold, you can use neoprene paddling gloves or pogies, the latter of which attach to the paddle and give your hands a warm place to grip the shaft.

If you decide that you're going to be paddling frequently in very cold weather, consider investing in a dry top or dry suit. These are expensive but give you excellent protection from inclement weather and low temperatures. A less expensive option is to get a neoprene wetsuit. These aren't as warm and comfortable as dry suits, but are much less expensive, and provide a reasonable amount of warmth and protection against cold water. These come in armless "farmer john/jane" styles, which are best for paddling.

MIXED CONDITIONS

The gray area when dressing for kayaking exists when the air temperature is warm but the water is cold. How do you avoid overheating but dress in preparation for unexpectedly winding up in the cold water? Unfortunately, there's no easy answer to this question. You need to be prepared for the possibility of capsizing. In the early spring just after the snow has melted where I live, I will overheat a bit during my workouts but I know how cold the water is, so it is worth the extra caution! Early spring is also when I am getting accustomed to being in a boat again; my balance can be off and my likelihood of accidentally dumping is at its highest. In the fall, don't misjudge water temperature. Especially in more northern climes, the days can be warm and beautiful, but bodies of water are usually cooling rapidly.

When the weather is warm but the water is cold, you should also exercise a little extra caution in deciding where and how you paddle. For example, avoid open water crossings and any other situation that puts you at risk of being in the water for a long period of time if you capsize. In these conditions, you should stay close to shore and paddle with someone who is also a competent paddler. Safety considerations for paddling in mixed conditions are discussed in more detail in Chapter 4: *Water Safety.*

Paddler's Check List

- ❏ **Boat**
- ❏ **Paddle**
- ❏ **Seat pad**
- ❏ **PFD**
- ❏ **Bilge pump**
- ❏ **Towline**
- ❏ **Whistle**
- ❏ **Light**
- ❏ **Watch**
- ❏ **Sunglasses**
- ❏ **Hat**
- ❏ **Water bottle**
- ❏ **Energy bar**

CHAPTER 2:
Before Hitting the Water

Old Town

Adventure XL 125

Kayak Maintenance and Storage

Kayaks are simple crafts and do not require a lot of maintenance. However, there are a few simple things you can do to prolong the life of your boat and keep it looking good.

The best thing you can do to prolong the life of your boat is to store it out of the sun. Over time, exposure to the sun will make plastic boats more brittle and composite boats more flexible (losing their rigidity compromises their performance). Ideally, your kayak should be stored in a cool, dry place, like a garage. If you have to store your boat outside, keep it in a shaded area and/or cover it with a tarp. You should also roll the kayak over on its side or completely upside-down to make sure rainwater can't get into the boat. Water is heavy and can easily warp or seriously damage your kayak if it is left inside for any length of time.

TIP

A good habit to get into is to rinse your boat with fresh water after each use—especially if you'll be using it in salt water. Pay particular attention to any moving parts like steering cables, rudders and skegs to be sure they are free of debris. It's also not a bad idea to wipe your boat down with an old towel as soon as you get out of the water, to remove dirt, scum and weeds picked up during your paddle before they dry and stick to the hull. You can also use a little bit of acetone on a rag to remove some marks and stains.

In an ideal world, kayaks would only ever touch air and water. If this were possible, our kayaks would last an eternity.

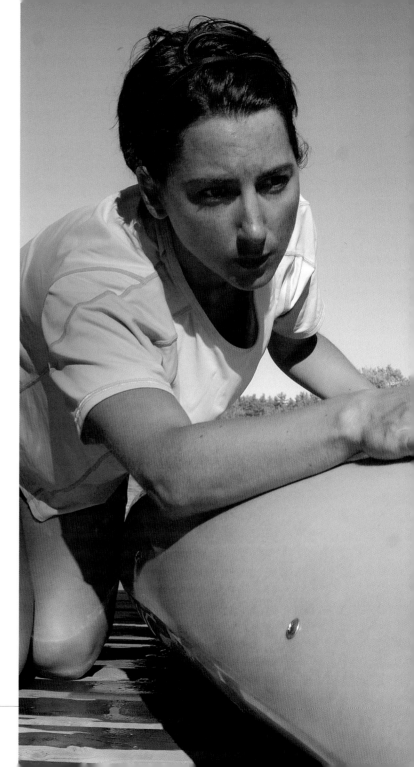

Unfortunately, bumps, dings and scratches are inevitable. Minor injuries are generally pretty easy to deal with. But what about when something major happens?

With enough force, it is possible to crack or puncture a kayak. You might be surprised to learn that the most serious injuries to kayaks occur while they are being transported. I cannot count the number of boats I have seen damaged this way. Even when boats have been tied down properly, roof racks have come off and boat trailers have flipped over. Amazingly, plastic boats often escape these events relatively unharmed but composite boats do not fare as well. Major cracks involving structural damage to the hull require full repair before going out on the water again. Fortunately, this type of damage can usually be taken care of by someone experienced in fiberglass work.

SPECIAL CARE FOR **COMPOSITE** KAYAKS

For composite boats, a good marine wax will protect it from the sun and from salt water if that's what you're dealing with. These polishes can be picked up at your local paddling store and they really bring back the shine on a boat's finish.

SPECIAL CARE FOR **PLASTIC** KAYAKS

With plastic boats it is very unlikely you will face any major repair and you'll be able to handle the small ones easily by yourself.

Scratches in the bottom of your boat are nothing to worry about, unless they are so deep that they go almost right through the hull. I like to think of each scratch as an individual record of all the good times I've had in my kayak. If you do want to clean up the bottom of your boat, your best bet is to use a razor blade to remove any strings of plastic that may be hanging off.

The major problem with plastic boats is their tendency to deform over time. This is usually caused by the sun's heat, your boat being stored in the same position for long periods of time or being tied down during transportation. It's important to know that unless the deformity is severe, it really doesn't affect the boat's performance and shouldn't be a cause for concern. If the boat is showing serious warping or dents, simply place your kayak upside-down in the sun on a hot day and allow heat to build inside it—this can miraculously eliminate many hull distortions. Another method is to fill the distorted area with hot water. The combination of the water's weight and the heat is usually enough to pop a plastic boat back into shape.

Transporting Your Kayak

Because most serious damage to kayaks takes place during transportation, reading and taking heed as prescribed in this next section might save you a boat or two!

First of all, I am a big fan of high-quality and professionally-installed roof racks. Unfortunately, roof racks that come with a vehicle, factory-installed, are not ideal. Manufacturers like Yakima or Thule specialize in roof racks and make kayak-specific attachments such as kayak rollers and cradles that do a great job of protecting your boat, and which also make loading and tying the kayaks safer and easier. Good roof racks can be fairly expensive but they protect your boat and can save your back.

If you are using basic bar racks, it's a good idea to pad the racks with foam to save your kayak some scratches and wear. You can use the same foam sleeping pad that you used to make your seat pad in Chapter 1. An even simpler way is to buy foam "pool noodles" with a hollow center, then slice them horizontally and fit them over the rack bars. These can then be fastened in place with good old duct tape or quick (zip) ties.

Loading Your Boat

It is possible for one person to load a boat up onto the rack on their own, but it is much easier for two people lifting from each end. Kayak rollers make it easy to load your boat if you are alone. From the back of the vehicle, you can lift one end of the kayak up onto the rollers and then move to the other end and slide the boat forward until it is resting perfectly in place.

To secure your boat to the roof rack, ropes work well enough, but if you are like my buddy Neil who has been paddling for years but can't tie a knot to save his life, cam straps are quicker and easier to use. You can get cam straps at any paddling or outdoor store. Regardless of what method you choose, securely tying a boat onto a roof rack is pretty easy if you follow these general guidelines:

- **Center the boat on the racks and tie the boat down in two places, one forward of center, the other behind center. As long as you don't strap the boat down at its widest point, your kayak will not be able to fly off.**

- **If you've got a plastic boat, don't be afraid to aggressively tighten ropes or straps; the chances of hurting your boat are slim.**

- **If you've got a composite or thermoformed kayak, a more delicate touch is appropriate. Pull until the rope or strap is tight, and then apply a little bit of pressure while you tie the knot or secure the cam strap.**

An added piece of insurance is to tie a bowline and stern line from your kayak to the front and back of your vehicle. If you do this, do not tie the lines too tightly or you risk bending your boat along its length which can stress or even damage your kayak's structural integrity. These lines are designed to be insurance against the boat flying forward or backward off the kayak.

As a final note, knots and cam straps do loosen over time, especially in wet conditions. On longer drives, get in the habit of pulling over to check that your boat is still securely tied down.

Carrying Your Kayak

When you carry your boat over land, remember the ideal that your kayak would only ever touch air and water. If your boat is too heavy to carry by yourself, get your paddling buddy to help. It is often easy for two people to carry two boats at the same time. It's a bit like hauling grocery bags, where having one kayak handle in each hand creates a balanced load. If it's not too heavy, place your gear in the cockpit to save making two trips.

If you have the strength to do it, you can carry a sit-inside kayak on your shoulder. To get the kayak on your shoulder, bend your legs and keep your back as straight as possible. Lift the boat onto your thighs, cockpit facing away from you. Next, grab the far edge of the cockpit coaming. In one smooth movement, kick the boat up with your knee and roll it onto your shoulder. To put the kayak back down, simply reverse these steps. If you don't have far to go and your boat isn't too heavy, you can also carry a boat like a suitcase from the center of the cockpit.

If for some reason you need to carry a kayak by yourself, you can get away with dragging a plastic kayak to the water; but you must never drag a composite or thermoformed boat. Even with a plastic kayak, you should really avoid dragging it over hard surfaces or you'll quickly wear out the hull. The best solution is to get a kayak cart. A kayak cart is a cradle with two wheels that supports one end of the kayak and allows just about anyone to pull the boat along from the other end. Most carts can be disassembled to be stored in a reasonably small space. Many can even fit inside the boat while you paddle.

1. Lift the kayak onto your thighs with the cockpit out.

2. Grab the far edge, thumb out, with the hand that is on the same side as the shoulder that the boat will sit on.

3. Use your knee to kick the boat up and roll it up onto your shoulder.

4. Don't forget to make wide turns when carrying a boat solo.

A kayak cart is a great way to carry a kayak by yourself.

Getting In and Out of Your Kayak

The most difficult part about getting into a kayak is the transition from standing beside the boat to getting your butt onto the seat.

The easiest place to get into a boat is from a low dock or a smooth beach. Higher docks make the transition process a little more difficult. The trick to getting into a kayak from a dock is to start by sitting down alongside your boat with your paddle close by so that it will be easy to reach once you're in. You'll then place your feet along the centerline of the kayak and quickly lower yourself down into the boat.

On a sandy beach, place your kayak completely in the water, straddle it with a foot on either side and then sit down. If you're paddling a plastic kayak, you also have the option of getting in with your boat on shore and then pushing yourself out with your hands.

For awkward or rocky launch sites, the best way to get into your boat involves floating your kayak in the water alongside the shoreline, and then using your paddle as an outrigger for support. Place your paddle at ninety degrees to the kayak with the shaft resting on the boat just behind the cockpit, and the far blade supported on shore. Grasp the paddle shaft and coaming behind your back, and squat down beside the kayak. Cheating your weight onto the outrigger, slip your legs into the boat and drop your butt into the seat. You can get out of your kayak on uneven or rocky shorelines using this same technique in reverse, although it will be more difficult if you have any waves to contend with.

For awkward or rocky launching sites, float your kayak parallel to shore and use your paddle as an outrigger for support on shore as you get on board.

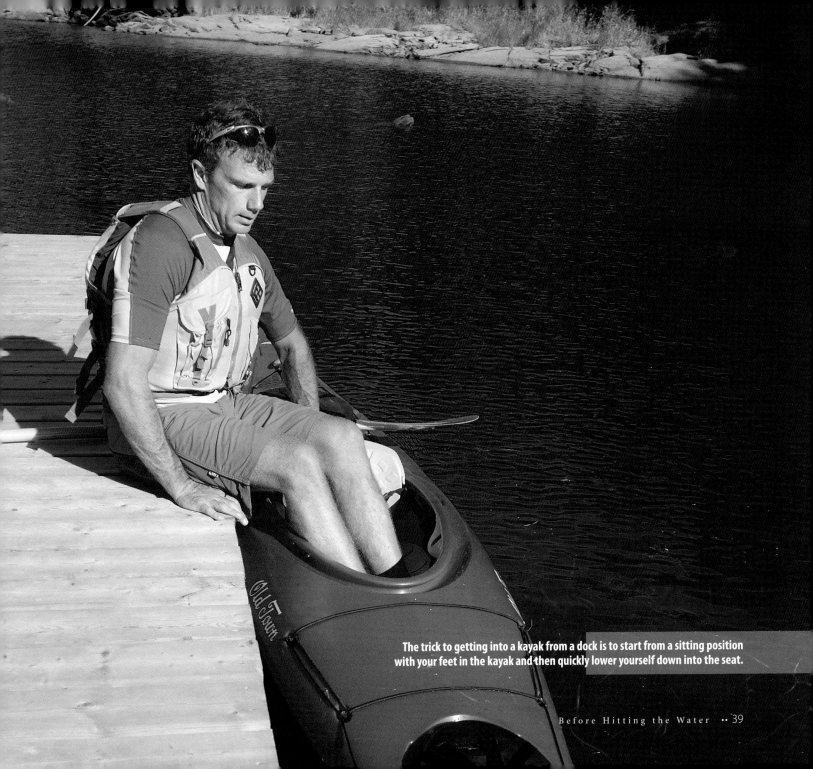

The trick to getting into a kayak from a dock is to start from a sitting position with your feet in the kayak and then quickly lower yourself down into the seat.

PUTTING ON A SPRAY SKIRT

If you're using a sit-inside kayak, you have the option of using a spray skirt. As we discussed in the equipment section, for the purpose of fitness kayaking, a simple nylon skirt will work well and will be easier to get on and off than a neoprene skirt. Even still, putting on the skirt can be tricky in the beginning. The best way to get your skirt on is to start from the back. You'll then work the skirt under the coaming around to your hips, and then stretch it over the front of the coaming. Make sure that when you do this that you leave the rip cord out, because you'll need it to get the skirt off when the time comes to get out.

If you're using a neoprene skirt and having trouble getting it on, try wetting it first. If you still can't get it on, then it's probably fair to say that it's not the right skirt for you.

Sitting In Your Kayak

The ideal sitting position in a kayak is upright. From there, arch your back slightly and push your navel to the front of the boat. Feel your pelvis roll forward, your spine grow taller and your vertebrae stack up one on top of the other. This is a slightly more aggressive paddling posture than you'd use when paddling recreationally, but for a fitness-focused workout, it gives you more balance and full power without risk of injury.

Tight hamstrings can limit how upright you can sit. Start stretching them regularly and you will see improvements surprisingly quickly. This stretching can also help you to avoid lower back pain.

Your feet should be firmly pressed against the foot pedals and your knees should be slightly bent. Some sit-inside kayaks will have thigh hooks that your legs should fit comfortably under. As you push on one foot brace at a time, you should be able to straighten your leg and allow your upper body to rotate naturally with this movement. If you can't straighten your leg with this pushing movement, move your foot pedals a little further back.

Using Your Paddle

The paddle translates your energy into forward acceleration, direction changes, stopping and turning, and over time, it will start to feel like an extension of your body. We've already discussed how to choose a paddle, so now let's look at how to use it.

If you are using a feathered paddle, you need to identify your control hand. In general, your dominant hand will be your control hand. This control hand keeps a firm (but light) grip on the paddle shaft at all times, whether you're forward paddling, back paddling or performing any other stroke. Your other hand is often referred to as the grease hand, and while you'll still use it to grip the shaft, it will loosen to allow the paddle shaft to rotate a bit with each stroke.

If you are using a paddle with no feather, you won't need to worry about rotating the shaft between each stroke; just grip the paddle shaft with both hands and go. Many people find this more intuitive and natural. As was mentioned beforehand, the only benefit to using a feathered paddle is that it cuts down the wind resistance acting on the airborne blade as you take a stroke. Try it both ways and go with what feels most comfortable for you.

To figure out how far apart your hands should be, hold your paddle horizontally on top of your head. Adjust where you grip the paddle shaft so that both arms are bent at the elbow at an angle of approximately ninety degrees and an equal distance from the blades. This hand placement gives you the best combination of control and power. Your grip on the paddle shaft should be light but secure, because a light grip will let you paddle more comfortably for longer, and will help you avoid overuse injuries such as tendonitis in the wrist.

With your hands an equal distance from the blades and your paddle on top of your head, your arms should be bent at 90 degrees.

If the right hand is the control hand, it should retain a firm grip with the big knuckles aligned with the top edge of the paddle blade.

The left hand stays loose so that after a stroke on the right is taken, the shaft can rotate in the left hand so the left blade can be planted squarely in the water.

Wet Exit

A wet exit is how you get out of a capsized boat quickly and safely. It is a skill that only really needs to be considered by those who are paddling sit-inside touring or sea kayaks, because if you flip while paddling a recreational kayak, you'll simply fall out. The wet exit is the first skill that anyone paddling a touring or sea kayak should learn, because the cockpit is so much smaller. Even though it's not difficult, until you've done it you'll probably remain nervous about the idea of flipping.

If you're wearing a spray skirt, always make sure that the rip cord is out, and not tucked inside the boat when you pull the skirt over the coaming. Once you've flipped, the first thing to do is lean forward and find this rip cord. Pull the rip cord to pop your skirt off the coaming, then slide your hands back to your hips, stay leaning forward and push yourself out. You'll end up doing a bit of a forward roll out of your boat and you'll be at the surface in no time.

The trickiest part of this maneuver is fighting the instinct to lean back as you slide out of your kayak. The problem with leaning back is that it raises your butt off the seat and presses your thighs against the thigh hooks, which will only slow you down. Remember to lean forward and you'll slide out easily.

The entire process of wet exiting will only take a few seconds and the more relaxed you are, the more smoothly it will all go. Once you're out, grab your boat and paddle to speed up the rescue process.

Practice the wet exit with a buddy who can be there for safety while you're figuring it out. Learning to wet exit is much easier than learning to ride a bicycle, but the same rule holds true—once you've learned it, you won't forget.

The wet exit only needs to be considered by those paddling sit-inside touring or sea kayaks, which have small cockpits.

Using Rudders or Skegs

Believe it or not, the main purpose of rudders and skegs isn't to turn a kayak, but to keep a kayak tracking (going straight) when paddling in wind. This is because a kayak will naturally want to turn into the wind, something that's called weathercocking. The rudder or skeg counteracts this tendency. Paddling in wind without a rudder or skeg can mean that you have to take much harder strokes on one side to keep your kayak tracking.

Rudders are much more popular than skegs because they can also be used to help steer a kayak. Rudders flip down from their stored position on top of the deck, through the use of haul lines found alongside the cockpit, and are then controlled using foot pedals.

TIP

If your boat didn't come with a rudder but you expect that you'll be paddling in windy conditions, consider getting one. Many kayaks now come with a rudder mount in the stern to allow for this option. If there is a rudder mount, you can have a rudder installed anytime that you decide that you need one.

Skegs are stored in a skeg box that is embedded in the stern of the kayak and they are deployed by using a slider found alongside the cockpit. Because skegs don't swivel side-to-side, their control comes from the depth at which they are set. The more your kayak wants to wants to weathercock, the deeper you will set the skeg. Skegs are really only useful for tracking over long distances, so you generally don't find them on recreational kayaks, but some sea and touring kayak models will come with them.

Edging Your Kayak

Edging your kayak is a great skill to learn as it will build your comfort level and will let you turn recreational or touring kayaks more easily than if they were sitting flat on the water. It becomes an even more important skill if you ever decide to take your paddling to the next level, as it lets you stay balanced when dealing with waves.

The key to edging your kayak is to stay loose at the hips and let your upper and lower body work independently but cooperatively. Keeping your body upright, shift your weight slightly over onto one butt cheek. You should feel your whole rib cage shifting over to the side of your kayak and your stomach and side muscles will be working a little bit to keep your body upright as you do so.

Edging is even easier if your kayak has thigh hooks, because your knees can then fine-tune the boat tilt. If your kayak doesn't have thigh hooks, no problem. You'll simply need to be more conservative with how much you edge your kayak.

Rudders are controlled by your foot pedals and are convenient to have on longer kayaks.

When they're needed, rudders flip down from their stored position on top of the deck and are controlled by your foot pedals. Contrary to popular belief, their main purpose is not to turn a kayak, but to help a kayak run straight in windy or wavy conditions.

Paddling Forward on Edge

Once you're comfortable with putting your kayak on a small edge while sitting still on flat water, it's a great idea to learn how to forward paddle with your boat on edge. Not only will it improve your balance and confidence in your kayak, but it will help work some of the important stabilizing muscles in your abdomen, making you a stronger paddler overall. The trick is to shift your weight onto a single butt cheek by shifting your whole rib cage over to one side, while at the same time keeping your head up and balanced over your kayak.

A great drill for working on this is to paddle in a straight line, switching from one edge to the other with about 10 strokes in a row on each side. In the early stages, don't worry about getting your boat on a hard edge. Focus more on simply shifting your weight and balancing on a single butt cheek. As you become more comfortable doing this, start gradually holding your kayak on a more aggressive edge.

As mentioned in the previous section on *Edging Your Kayak*, edging is easier if your kayak has thigh hooks, but if it doesn't, it's not a problem. Simply be a little more conservative about how far you put your boat on edge.

CHAPTER 3:
Essential Strokes

While kayaking is generally very intuitive, there are some key strokes that are worth taking the time to learn properly because they'll allow you to travel on the water most efficiently and maneuver more effectively. To begin, we're going to take a thorough look at the forward stroke because it is the most important stroke to learn for fitness kayaking. Following this, we'll take a quick look at a few other key kayaking strokes, but if you're really interested in developing your boat handling skills, there are some great books and DVDs available to help you—not to mention the immense value of on-water instruction.

Forward Stroke

For the purpose of fitness kayaking, all paddlers should learn an efficient and powerful forward stroke because with it, you'll be able to paddle faster and longer. A proper forward stroke also engages more muscle groups and will give you a better full body workout.

Over the years as a coach, personal trainer and instructor, I have discovered an easy system to develop powerful, efficient strokes quickly. I break the stroke down into four components: wind-up, catch, power phase, and exit/set-up.

WIND-UP

Beginner paddlers are often surprised to learn that the power for a good forward stroke does not come from the arms; it comes from the torso and legs, harnessed through body rotation. Think of your body as an elastic band. Rotating your body is how you'll wind it up; and the more you wind it up, the more power you'll get from it. For the forward stroke, you'll wind your body up and then plant the paddle in the water at your toes.

Proper rotation is the single most important component in any kayak stroke as it allows the paddler to engage larger muscle groups, including those of the back and the abdomen but also the larger muscles of the legs, like your glutes and hamstrings. When you paddle, try to focus on these larger muscle groups more than the smaller muscle groups of the arms. Your biceps and triceps will get their share of work either way.

We're going to start developing your body rotation on dry land with an exercise I call "Paddling With Your Butt". The idea here is to "walk" forward on your butt cheeks. Start by sitting on the grass in a good upright paddling position. Now bring your whole right side forward including your right butt cheek and hip. Make your shoulders and hips move as one unit. Now shift your weight onto the right butt cheek. You'll now repeat this process, but you'll bring the whole left side of your body forward as a unit. You'll then shift your weight onto the left butt cheek. Continue the alternating motions so that you are basically "walking" on your butt cheeks. The purpose of this exercise is to get the feeling of using the lower body as well as the upper body to propel you forward.

Now to take this one step further, place a garbage bag or some other slippery material under you and have a friend kneel down in front of you. Place your feet against their knees and have them hold your feet in place with their hands. Try to imagine a pole that you are straddling coming up out of the ground right in front of you. Now try rotating your hips around this imaginary pole—first one side and then the other—by pushing and pulling with your legs against your friend. One butt cheek will move forward as the other moves back. Make sure that your upper body is working as a unit with the lower body. You should feel this same push and pull movement when you are paddling, powering the boat forward with your legs from the rotation of the hips, as well as from the back and upper torso. Really exaggerate this exercise by reaching forward with a relaxed front shoulder and arm.

CATCH

The catch is the moment when you place the paddle blade in the water, before you exert any pressure on it. The ideal catch is planted as far ahead as you can reach and sinks the blade fully in the water.

Be careful that you don't unwind before the blade has been fully immersed, which shortchanges you of several inches of the stroke's potential length. Because the kayak stroke is quite short, losing even a little bit of reach at the beginning of your stroke means that a lot of the potential energy stored up in your rotation will be lost.

Winding up for a forward stroke means rotating your body before planting your stroke. This lets you engage the large muscles of your back, abdomen and legs.

To achieve a good catch, use your bottom hand to reach the blade as far forward as possible alongside the boat and then use your top hand to push the blade down forcefully into the water. Let the pushing forward movements of your lower hand, arm and shoulder feel fairly relaxed, but let the movement of your top hand be more aggressive so it feels the pressure of the catch first. Timing here is very important to get the most power. You must pause for just a millisecond to allow the top hand to fully submerge the blade before you begin your stroke. Keep in mind that this pause should be very short and flow with the rest of your stroke.

TIP

If you get a chance, have someone take video footage of you paddling from the side. Look for the moment that the blade has fully disappeared underwater—your upper body should not be moving at all, except to apply downward force to the submerging blade.

A good catch involves fully submerging the blade before pulling on it.

Here is a technical drill to help you keep your body in the right position. Stick your top hand to your forehead during each stroke. The only way you can get the blade to move through the water with your hand stuck here is with body rotation. If you have a tendency to push forward with the top hand, you will find it difficult to keep this position but it will help you break the habit.

POWER PHASE

The power phase is when you exert pressure on the paddle blade to push the boat forward through the water. Power comes from un-winding from your rotation and is therefore delivered by the big muscle groups in your legs and torso. Your arms will naturally be involved because they are holding onto your paddle, but avoid any extra pulling or pushing with your hands. Your arms should actually stay in a relatively fixed position from the catch through the power phase.

Let's pick up where we left off with the catch. Your top hand has just pushed your blade down and into the water. Your top arm will be bent at the elbow at about 90 degrees, and remain bent at this angle which will allow you to keep the blade in the best position in the water and allow full use of your rotation. Now, push with your leg (the one that's on the same side as your active blade) as you unwind and rotate in the other direction. Remember that your hips and shoulders should move forward as one unit. As you do this, your top hand will cross over the center line of the boat to help keep your paddle shaft vertical throughout the stroke.

EXIT/SET-UP

The exit is the moment of removing the paddle blade from the water, it should transition seamlessly into the wind-up for the next stroke on the other side.

As your bottom hand passes your knee and approaches your hips at the end of the power phase, begin raising the blade out of the water. The blade should be fully out of the water by the time your bottom hand is in line with your hip.

With your blade out of the water, your body should already be well into the wind-up phase for the next stroke. Continue rotating your body and reach the forward hand as far towards the bow as possible. You're now ready to use your top hand to push that next blade down forcefully into the water to catch water for your next stroke.

The stroke ends and your blade should be fully out of the water by the time your bottom hand is in line with your hip.

Reverse Stroke

You'll probably find that you naturally don't need to back paddle very often, but as a fitness tool it is definitely worth developing a comfortable reverse stroke. We will be incorporating it into the fitness program to help develop a more balanced body by working the opposite muscle groups. This will also help to avoid injury and you can use it to get out of tight situations and avoid potential collisions.

Quite simply, the reverse stroke is the same as the forward stroke, only in reverse. There is no need to change your grip because the reverse stroke uses the back of the paddle blade. Simply rotate your body, place the blade in the water just behind your hip and then unwind to push the blade toward the bow of the boat. When the stroke reaches the end of its line, your body should be wound up and in a position to plant the other blade just behind your hip for a reverse stroke on

1. Rotating your upper body aggressively, the reverse stroke gets planted fully in the water just behind your hip.

2. Notice the arms stay in a relatively fixed position, because torso rotation provides the bulk of the power for the stroke.

3. The reverse stroke ends when your blade reaches your toes.

4. Remember that you'll keep the same grip on your paddle, which means the reverse stroke uses the back of your paddle blade.

the other side. As with the forward stroke, the power for the reverse stroke comes from your body rotation—not from pushing and pulling with your arms.

Take a glance over your shoulder every few strokes to check where you're going. It is easiest to do so over the same shoulder that reaches back when planting your reverse stroke behind the hip.

Stopping

Even though one of your goals as a fitness paddler is to improve the efficiency with which you can go forward, it is also essential to know how to stop quickly. It's easy to miss seeing a submerged log or rock until the last second. In this case, the best way to stop is with braking strokes, which are short, quick, alternating reverse strokes with the blade fully submerged into the water at your hips. You should be able to come to a complete stop with just two or three of these strokes.

Sweep Strokes

Virtually all kayaks, with the exception of whitewater kayaks, are designed to travel well in a straight line. Although this is usually a helpful attribute, when it comes to turning, these kayaks are less than responsive. The only effective way to do so is through the use of sweep strokes. There are both forward and reverse sweep strokes to choose from, and both can be used while stationary or moving.

1. **The forward sweep starts with your body wound up and your paddle planted deeply at your toes with the shaft held low.**

2. **Keeping your hands low, sweep an arcing path far out to the side of the kayak.**

3. **Follow your active blade with your eyes to help incorporate torso rotation into the stroke.**

4. **Finish your sweep before your paddle hits the stern of your kayak.**

FORWARD SWEEP

The forward sweep stroke is a great way to turn while still traveling forward, because it allows you to maintain your speed.

The forward sweep starts very much like the forward stroke: with your body rotated and your blade completely submerged in the water at your toes. Unlike the forward stroke, however, your top hand will stay lower and will help guide your blade through a wide arc as far out to the side of your kayak as possible. It shouldn't come as any surprise by this point that the power for the forward sweep comes from your body rotation. To encourage your body rotation, try watching the active blade throughout the stroke and push off the foot pedal on the sweeping-stroke side of the boat. You can also think about pushing the front of your boat away from the blade during the first half of the sweep and pulling the stern toward the blade in the second half.

When finishing the stroke, be sure to pull the blade out of the water before it touches the stern. Otherwise, your blade can get pinned against the boat and throw you off balance.

REVERSE SWEEP

The reverse sweep is exactly what it sounds like—a forward sweep stroke done in reverse. Like the back stroke, you'll use the back face of your paddle so there is no need to change your grip on the shaft. The reverse sweep can be used while stationary or when traveling forward, although it's important to note that in the latter situation, it will kill almost all of your speed. It can be a very useful stroke when you need to put on the brakes and make a major course correction at the same time.

The wind up for the reverse sweep involves turning your upper body aggressively and watching your paddle enter the water at the stern of your kayak. Both hands should stay low—one reaching out over the water and the other taking position in front of your stomach. With your blade planted deeply in the water, sweep a full, wide arc all the way out to the side of your kayak and then to your toes. While doing so, watch the active blade's progression and aggressively unwind your body.

Try this exercise with the boat stationary: combine a forward sweep on one side with a reverse sweep on the opposite side. You'll find this combination of strokes will spin your kayak more or less right on the same spot.

1. **The reverse sweep starts at the stern of your kayak with your head and body aggressively rotated towards it.**

2. **Keeping your hands low, sweep a wide arc with your paddle.**

3. **Notice the arms have stayed in a relatively fixed position throughout the stroke, which means torso rotation is providing much of the power.**

4. **The stroke ends after having swept a full, wide arc.**

SWEEPING ON EDGE

As was mentioned in the section on *Edging Your Kayak*, putting your kayak on edge lets it turn more easily. So, once you're comfortable sweeping with your boat kept flat, it's time to add some boat tilt to the equation to make your sweep stroke its most effective. Whether you're using a forward or reverse sweep stroke, you'll tilt your kayak on edge towards your active sweeping blade.

① ② ③ ④

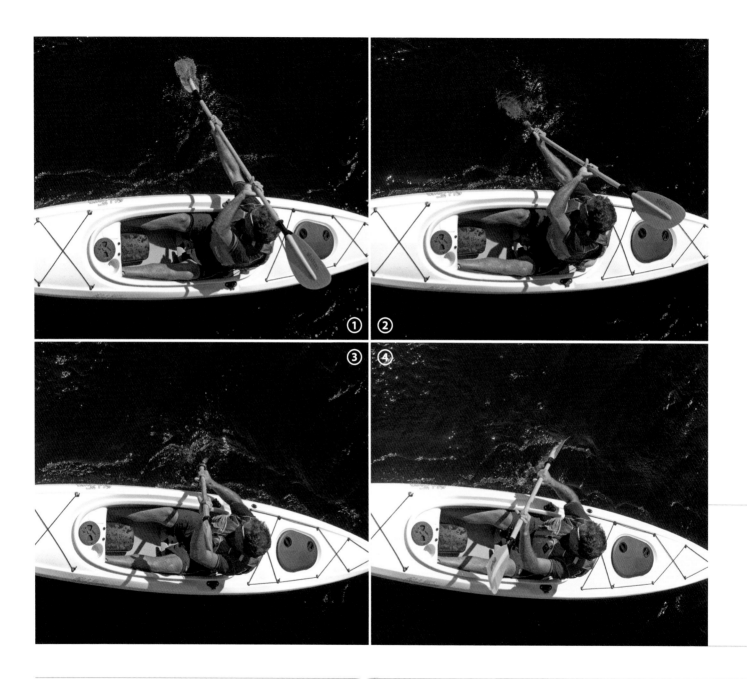

Draw Stroke

Draw strokes are used to move your kayak sideways, such as when you need to pull yourself up alongside shore or closer to your paddling partner.

The draw stroke is simple. It involves reaching out and planting your paddle completely in the water about two feet straight out from your hip, and then pulling that blade directly towards you to move the boat sideways.

To make the stroke the most efficient, rotate your head and upper body to face your active blade, and keep your paddle shaft as vertical as possible. Getting your paddle shaft vertical will require reaching across your upper body with your top hand, which takes good balance and is something for beginners to gradually work up to.

When your blade is completely in the water, pull your lower hand in towards your hip. Your top hand will stay very stationary, acting as the pivot point for the stroke. Before your paddle hits your boat, you'll need to finish the stroke by slicing the blade out of the water towards the stern. The paddle should exit about six inches away from the side. Be careful that you do not bring your paddle too close to the side of your kayak before finishing the stroke. As was the case with the forward sweep, if your paddle gets pinned up against the side your kayak, it can easily throw you off balance.

One of the most common problems people have with the draw stroke is that they find that it turns their kayak rather than moving it only sideways. If you experience this problem, it usually means that you're using your draw stroke too far forward or too far back. If you're pulling your draw too far forward (towards your knee instead of your hip) you'll pull your bow towards your paddle. If your draw is too far back, you'll pull your stern towards your paddle. Drawing your paddle towards your hip is a good guideline, but every kayak reacts differently and you can expect to need to make some fine adjustments to keep your boat moving perfectly sideways.

1. **With your head and upper body turned to face the active blade, plant the draw stroke about two feet straight out from your hip.**

2. **Pull the paddle directly toward you.**

3. **End the draw stroke before your paddle hits your boat.**

4. **Slice the paddle out of the water towards the stern of the kayak and you're ready for your next stroke.**

CHAPTER 4

Water Safety

> Re-entry

> Choosing a Good
Paddling Location

Compared to most other outdoor activities, kayaking is remarkably safe. Although the chances of getting hurt are very low, it is important to be aware that things can still go wrong. Any activity that takes place around water has the potential to lead to tricky situations that can quickly become serious dangers. However, with some basic knowledge, a safety-conscious attitude and good judgment, kayaking remains a low-risk way to stay in shape.

Staying safe on the water is largely about being aware of the hazards that exist in the area that you choose to paddle.

It's pretty easy to stay out of trouble in a kayak. The three most basic ways, which I almost shouldn't have to mention, are:

- **Never drink alcohol while on the water or paddle when intoxicated.**

- **Equip yourself with a PFD that fits you properly and wear it at all times.**

- **Always tell someone where you are going and when you plan to be back.**

Your first line of defense when heading out to paddle is your own judgment. This means you should only go out on the water when you are able to paddle safely and avoid what will put you at risk. Good gear is useful and sound paddling skills can help, but there is no substitute for common sense. Before you get on the water, look at the weather forecast, feel the water, consider where you are going to be paddling and stop to think about what the consequences of a mistake or problem would be. Even the most skilled, best-equipped and knowledgeable kayakers can run into problems. For example, your paddle could break, you could capsize, or fierce headwinds could whip up and prevent an easy return. Consider some of the risks and have plans for how to deal with them.

ONE SPRING, at the beginning of April, I wanted to get a run down a local river to prepare for an early season race. My friend Brian dropped me off upstream and we agreed that he was going to meet me several kilometers downstream at the end of my run. I had checked out the river from the road the day before and thought that it was completely open, but a few bends downstream after leaving Brian behind, the river opened up into a section of swamp that was still completely frozen over. The ice wasn't thick enough to hold my weight; with each step I crashed through. By the time I realized I'd horribly misjudged the state of the river, I was a long way from the road and had no choice but to continue down the river hopping in and out, and breaking through ice on frozen, tired legs.

After hours of painful, frigid and wet travel, I was still nowhere near the place where I was to meet Brian. I came across a railway line, and hoping for a way back to the road, I followed it through long stretches of wilderness. The sun set and by this time I was very cold. Suddenly, out of the blue, a young kid approached on a snowmobile. He took me several miles back to the road and the spot where I was to meet Brian. Although it was three hours late, my good friend Brian was still there.

Things were bad but they could have gone a lot worse: if I were less physically fit, if I were improperly dressed, if the boy on the snowmobile hadn't come along, if I didn't pack emergency snacks, and if I didn't have Brian waiting for me at the other end. I am thankful for some good measures of planning, but realize that it was stupid to head off on my own into such a risky situation. I definitely paid for this mistake; for several days it was almost too painful to walk due to the swelling in my lower legs from all the abuse and cold that they'd endured.

Re-entry

Even the best paddlers capsize sometimes. If you have a very stable boat, a great sense of balance, an easy place to launch and land, and never paddle in waves or wind, this might only happen once a decade—but it's safe to assume it will happen. It's nothing to be embarrassed about, and hopefully you took up kayaking because you like the water at least a little. However, the fact that you'll likely capsize at some point means that it's important to know how to get back into your boat from the water.

One of the huge advantages of sit-on-top kayaks is that they're easy to get back into from the water, which makes them a lot like small, high performance floating docks. In fact, many people will deliberately hop on and off sit-on-tops to swim on hot days. Sit-inside kayaks are more difficult to get back into from the water, but with a little instruction and some help from a friend, it can be done with relative ease.

RE-ENTRY FOR A SIT-ON-TOP KAYAK

To get back onto a sit-on-top from the water, get beside your boat next to the seat. You can keep your paddle in one hand, slide it under your deck lines so that it doesn't get away from you, or give it to someone to hold onto. With a firm grip on the kayak, let your legs float to the surface behind you. Then give a powerful kick with your legs and push with your arms to haul your chest up onto the kayak. Once you're up on the boat, twist your body around and settle into the seat, and then swing your legs back into position.

RE-ENTRY FOR A SIT-INSIDE KAYAK

Getting back into a sit-inside kayak from the water is a bit more complicated, not only because the boat will fill with water; the deck of the kayak is higher above the surface of the water, which means that you'll have a harder time climbing up on it, and it will be less stable once you're up there. Although it's possible to re-enter a sit-inside kayak on your own, it's one of those techniques that takes training and a lot of practice, and is not something we're going to look at in depth. What we're going to focus on instead is a way to re-enter a sit-inside kayak with the help of a friend.

The first order of business is to flip your boat upright if it's upside-down. When your boat is upside-down, air is trapped inside which keeps water from flooding the interior. This means that the quicker you can flip the boat upright, the less water will get scooped inside.

With the kayak upright, your paddling partner can stabilize the kayak as you get back in. A partner can actually provide an incredible amount of stability, although it requires a lot of commitment on his or her part. To stabilize someone's kayak, pull the boat in parallel to yours. Get a good grip on it and lean your whole body over onto it. As long as you have a

1. You'll need the help of a friend to re-enter a sit-inside kayak.

2. The rescuer gets a firm grip on the bow and leans their weight onto the empty boat to stabilize it while the swimmer re-enters.

3. Once the swimmer has pulled themselves on top of the kayak, they'll spin and drop their butt into the seat.

4. The rescuer needs to maintain their support of the swimmer's kayak throughout the re-entry.

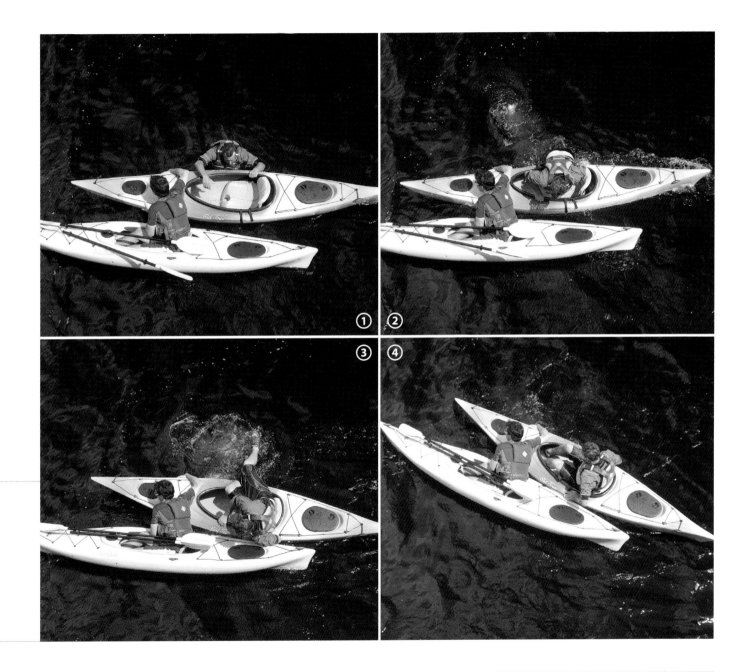

① ② ③ ④

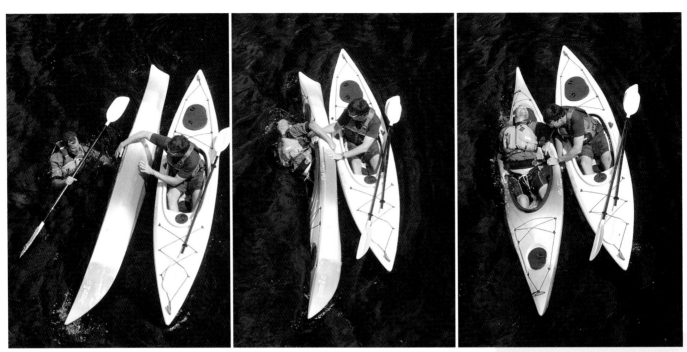

The scoop is a good rescue if the swimmer is unable to lift themselves out of the water.

good grip on the kayak, there's virtually no chance of flipping yourself. The swimmer can then hop back in using what is essentially the same re-entry technique described for the sit-on-top above.

To get back into a sit-inside that is being stabilized, get next to your boat just behind the seat and grab the cockpit rim, which conveniently provides a good handle. Let your legs float to the surface behind you and then with a powerful kick and push of your arms, haul your chest up and onto your stern deck. You'll then twist your body back into the seat. When you're done, you'll probably have a fair amount of water in the boat to deal with. You can either go right to shore to empty it out, or you can pump it out with your bilge pump.

The Scoop

If the person in the water finds that they don't have the strength or energy to haul themselves back into their boat, the scoop rescue might be the best option—unless you are close enough to shore that swimming or towing the overturned boat to shore is a better option. For the scoop, the swimmer must basically float back into the overturned, swamped kayak, and then rely on the paddling partner to haul them and the boat upright.

The rescuer stabilizes the boat as for a regular assisted sit-inside re-entry, but this time the boat will remain on its side, partially overturned and swamped. The swimmer then slides as far into the kayak as they can, and then leans all the way onto their stern deck, which lowers their center of gravity while the rescuer pulls up hard on the cockpit coaming to right the swamped kayak. Once they're upright, the rescuer needs to continue to stabilize their boat, because the boat will be full of water and need to be pumped out.

TIP

If you are interested in developing more advanced self-rescue skills, you may want to consider learning to roll your kayak. Rolling a kayak involves returning it to an upright position without exiting the boat after you capsize. Once you've got this skill, capsizing becomes very easy to recover from quickly—rolling is the fastest way to get your boat upright, and because you stay inside, you can just keep paddling! There are some very useful books on the subject that are terrific for understanding concepts, but a course is the quickest way to learn how to roll.

Choosing a Good Paddling Location

The ideal kayaking environment has a good access point for launching, multiple places to go ashore easily, shelter from wind and waves, and minimal motorized boating traffic.

It is useful to have a regular spot for training so that you can get familiar with the area. In Chapter 6, which outlines specific workouts, you'll see how getting to know an area means you can use the same measured-out sections for training exercises and to help chart your progress. However, it's also a good idea to have a few other locations scouted out so that you have places to choose from depending on the day's conditions. For example, a body of water that is ideal for paddling when the wind is westerly might be terrible for paddling when the wind is coming from the south or north.

TRAFFIC HAZARDS

Boat traffic on the water represents one of the greatest possible dangers to a kayaker. Kayaks are close to the water and not always easily visible, as well as being relatively slow moving and therefore unable to speed away from potential collisions. With motorized or other water traffic, always assume the worst: that they can't see you and don't know the rules of the water. Remember that in a collision with another

Paddling close to shore is always a wise thing to do because it offers a myriad of benefits for the recreational or fitness paddler. Along shorelines, water is often calmer and more protected; motorized vessels tend to stay away because the water is shallower; and if you accidentally capsize for any reason, it is easier to get to shore to empty your boat, which means it's safer and easier to paddle solo. The scenery is also often more interesting!

vessel, a kayak will always come out the loser. Even when you know you have the right of way, it is better to stay clear. Wear bright, reflective colors to increase your visibility, and seek out routes and locations that are as clear of boat traffic as possible. Stay aware of the movement of other boats in the area where you are paddling. Paddle close to shore and stick to more shallow water where most boats can't go.

Large and commercially-operated boats usually have a regular, established route, stick to deeper water and maneuver very predictably, so they're easier to avoid. These boats usually have trained professionals at the helm who tend to be more aware of other watercraft around them. The boats that are of greatest concern to the kayaker are the smaller, amateur-operated recreational boats. These boats often turn without warning, travel at high speeds in confined areas, and are unaware of other boats around them.

OCEAN HAZARDS

The ocean is a highly dynamic paddling environment and requires special consideration even if you plan to stick to protected channels. Fog, tides, currents and quickly-changing weather will all determine when and where it is safe to paddle. Get to know your area well and have several escape routes figured out in case conditions deteriorate quickly. Most importantly, get informed: take courses, read books about ocean kayaking, and get dependable advice from experienced local paddlers or guides.

In some areas, tidal currents can be very powerful. When I was a young and inexperienced paddler, I learned this the hard

way on a 4 mile (6 km) paddle to a place called Race Rocks. It took me 45 minutes to get there and hours of unexpectedly struggling against the current to get home. If I had equipped myself with more knowledge of the tides and currents, I could have better planned my trip.

Tides themselves cause water levels to rise and fall on the ocean, which can radically change the shoreline. Low tides can expose sharp, barnacle-covered rocks, cause channels to run dry, or reveal expansive mud flats that leave you stranded. High tides can cover beaches and swallow up potential landing or launch sites. Rising water can also catch the unwary paddler who leaves an unattended kayak on the shore too long, by picking up the boat and floating it away. The good news is that tides are predictable and well-documented! Check your local tidal schedules and study up-to-date marine charts of the area you want to paddle so that you are prepared for the conditions you'll encounter.

As always, the other rules of staying close to shore and selecting protected paddling locations will help you have a safe, fun training session on the ocean, and are essential to follow unless you have been trained and are comfortable with paddling in exposed open water conditions. Remember that when conditions start to deteriorate, the best course of action is always to get off the water quickly.

If you venture into water that is unprotected from wind and waves, it is imperative that you be trained and comfortable with a variety of rescue techniques. For more information about where you can get this training, visit your local outdoor or paddling shop.

I SPENT A YEAR living on Vancouver Island near Canada's west coast in my early twenties when I was attending university. The school and my living quarters were both on the ocean a few miles down the shore from each other. As soon as I could convince the school to give me a key to their boathouse, I began paddling to and from school routinely. This was how I became familiar with the power of the ocean. What was a perfectly glassy, flat water morning commute was often transformed into huge winds and swells for an epic afternoon trip home. Not only was launching in such conditions challenging, but finding a safe landing spot was also more difficult. My alternative route was to leave my boat in the boat house and run home along a beautiful beach if the paddling was too rough.

RIVER HAZARDS

Rivers can be great places to paddle, especially since in many cases you will rarely be far from shore and frequently be more protected from wind and large waves. A gentle current can also help your timing on downstream legs.

Current can also represent a formidable danger. Even a very light current can exert a surprisingly high amount of pressure on objects in its path. If you plan to paddle a section

Paddling in current can add some spice to your time on the water, but you should learn about it before you paddle in it to make sure you stay safe. As a general rule, it's a good idea to get professional instruction if you plan on paddling in anything more than light current.

of river, be sure to thoroughly investigate the area for potential hazards. If you have little knowledge or experience about paddling in current but plan to do so, I highly recommend that you take a basic whitewater paddling course to learn how to handle yourself in current.

Stationary obstacles in moving water are high-risk hotspots. While rocks and fallen trees can make navigating difficult, strainers are downright dangerous. A strainer is any obstacle that allows nothing but water to pass through it. Strainers can be created by a cluster of boulders (called boulder sieves) logjams, fallen trees, or dense bush and trees that have become partially or fully submerged. Strainers are dangerous because the moving water can sweep you into the impassable obstruction and then the force of the current can hold you pinned in place. If your head is trapped underwater and you get caught in a strainer, a rescuer will have only a short time to get you out. Do not underestimate the danger of strainers and simply avoid them at all costs.

Foot entrapment is another serious hazard. Many riverbeds consist of a jumble of rocks and other debris. If you trip and fall while wading in moving water, your foot can get trapped in place. The force of moving water—even if the current seems gentle—can make it surprisingly difficult or even impossible to free yourself from the foothold by yourself. The worst outcomes range from bone fracture to drowning. The safest way to avoid foot entrapment is to always swim if you're out of your boat and in moving water that is any higher than knee level. This may mean crawling those last few steps into shore instead of standing up, but a bump on the knee is far better than the worst things that can happen if you get your foot stuck.

Weather can blow in very quickly, and so it's important that you keep an eye on the sky. In particular, fog and lightning are real hazards for paddlers.

WEATHER HAZARDS

Weather obviously has a huge bearing on when and where you should go kayaking. Winds can come up quickly without warning and make handling your kayak significantly more difficult. With wind come waves. Waves are another serious hazard which can also result from boat traffic. The best strategy to remain stable in waves is to paddle into them head on. If this is not possible, try to stay relaxed, keep paddling, and allow the boat to sway freely underneath you, letting your hips rock with the boat and keeping your torso loose.

Fog can also seriously affect a kayaker's ability to safely travel on the water. Being enveloped in fog is eerie and disorienting. It's easy to feel completely stripped of any sense of direction and become hopelessly lost. In many locations, fog is seasonal or occurs in accordance with certain prevailing weather patterns. It may also be more common in the mornings or evenings. Fog can roll in quickly, obscuring landmarks and blotting out reference points, so be wary of it and avoid getting caught out. At the first sign of fog forming, turn around, head for home and hug the shore.

Rain is not a problem when you're out in a kayak; paddling in the rain can be quite pleasant. However, thunder and lightning are another matter. Thunder signals the approach of a lightning storm. Lightning is very, very dangerous for anyone out on the water. Bobbing on the surface of the water, you sitting in your kayak can easily become the highest point for quite a distance in any direction, making you a natural lightning rod. At the first hint of thunder or lightning, get off the water immediately. It is also wise to wait for at least thirty minutes after thunder and lightning have passed through before you go out on the water again.

CHAPTER 5:

Fitness & Training

Principles of Training

Proper training alternates physical stress with physical rest. The physical stress of a workout damages cells; the physical rest allows the cells to heal and your body to grow stronger and more efficient. This process is called **adaptation.** The key to building strength and fitness is to keep physical stress within reasonable limits and to support your recovery with proper rest, nutrition and care. Some of the physiological benefits gained from training include increased circulation, respiratory function, strength and power, as well as more resilient tendons, ligaments and bones.

Overloading is the most basic principle of fitness and refers to the increased physical demand placed on the body to force adaptation. The load is changed in a systematic manner by altering the frequency (how often), duration (how long), or the intensity (how hard) of each training session. If the training load is not great enough there will be little or no increase in fitness level or athletic performance. The overload must continue in a progressive manner. If a training program stays at the same intensity for an extended period of time, adaptations will only be evident at the beginning; after this the body will no longer be overloaded and will cease to adapt and improve.

Targeting is also important. This means that your training must be specific to the exercise or movements that you seek to improve. For example, if you don't spend any time in a boat then you will never get faster or more efficient as a kayaker no matter how much weight you can lift or how far you can run.

Rest and recovery are often the most overlooked principles of training. It is during the recovery periods that the positive physical adaptations to overloading occur. Recovery does not necessarily mean spending time on the couch. More often it means gentle training sessions of lower intensity or shorter duration that do not increase the stress placed on your body. These recovery sessions are usually terrific opportunities to focus on your technique.

Over-training is the term for when an individual becomes excessively fatigued due to too much overloading, repeating the same workout too many times, or not getting sufficient recovery. Classic signs of over-training are:
• Decreases in performance
• Aches and pains in muscles and joints
• Fatigue and insomnia
• Elevated morning pulse
• Headaches
• Inability to complete training sessions
• Susceptibility to illness

Variation will help you to avoid over-training and under-training. Because training is a long-term process, variety will keep things interesting, stave off boredom and keep you inspired to keep getting out there. Variation can include cross-training, alternating the hard and easy training days, and rest days.

The expression "use it or lose it" applies to your fitness as well. During a period of inactivity your body will quickly lose its fitness. This process is called **reversibility.** With endurance training, the benefits achieved are unfortunately lost more quickly than they are gained, so it's a great idea to keep up with regular workouts. Let exercise become part of your lifestyle and reap the benefits year-round.

Understanding Aerobic and Anaerobic Training

Think of your body as an engine that can burn three different types of fuel. The first is *adenosine triphosphate*, or ATP. You will have to go back to your high school biology notes to remember exactly how this stuff works, but simply put, it is free energy. It is like turning on the afterburners on a jet aircraft: it's very powerful stuff, but it only lasts for under a minute.

At the other end of the spectrum is the body fat that you can use for fuel. To burn fat, your body requires oxygen. Training at this level is called **aerobic.** Physically, aerobic training delivers a lot of benefits to your body. It increases your blood volume, increases the amount of oxygen your body can transport to your muscles, and strengthens your heart and lungs. Aerobic training gets your entire cardio-respiratory system to consume, absorb, and transport more oxygen, more efficiently. With this kind of training, your body will be able to increasingly sustain periods of high intensity training and allow you to gradually handle more challenging workouts. Long-distance running is an example of mostly aerobic exercise.

In between burning ATP and burning fat, your engine can also burn sugars. The system that allows your body to use sugar as a fuel without the use of oxygen is referred to as your lactic or **anaerobic** system. You can go really hard when using your anaerobic system for power. Unfortunately there is potential to overdo it here. Lactic acid is one by-product of burning sugar without enough oxygen. Lactic acid builds up in your blood and creates a burning sensation in your muscles, eventually resulting in deep muscular fatigue. Sprint-distance running is mostly anaerobic exercise.

HEART RATE ZONES

Different levels of exertion can be calculated based on your heart rate during exercise. These levels are classified in zones from 1 to 5, easiest to most difficult. With or without a heart rate monitor (HRM), it's a good idea to know how hard you are exercising based on your heart rate so that you can optimize your training. For the exercise program in this book, I've referred to these zones to help you gauge your exertion levels.

TIP

If you have just started working out, consider it optional to measure your heart rate—your main focus should be on enjoying the different training sessions and getting into an exercise routine. There are other more casual but reasonably effective ways to gauge exertion levels that do not require measuring heart rates, like the talk test which is described later in this chapter.

You can easily calculate how hard you are training based on your heart rate.

Let's start with the **resting heart rate (RHR),** which is a good measure of general fitness. If you're curious about this, you can start monitoring your pulse first thing in the morning. After a few days you will have a pretty good idea of your current RHR. As your fitness improves over time, your RHR will drop slightly. An increase in resting heart rate can indicate that your body has not fully recovered from previous exercise. A continual climb in these readings can indicate over-training, too little rest, or that your body is fighting something like an illness or infection. Under these circumstances, it can be a good idea to go for a "junk paddle" where you basically just relax with a short tour on the water, or take the day off entirely.

To find out what your personal training zones are, you must first calculate your **maximum heart rate (MHR),** which is different for everyone. Heart rates are measured in beats per minute. If you do not have a heart rate monitor, you can feel your pulse and count it for 10 or 15 seconds. (If you count it for 10 seconds, simply multiply the total by 6; if you count it for 15 seconds, multiply the total by 4 to determine your heart rate.) If you have a heart rate monitor, the manufacturer probably provided specific instructions for how to use the device to determine your MHR.

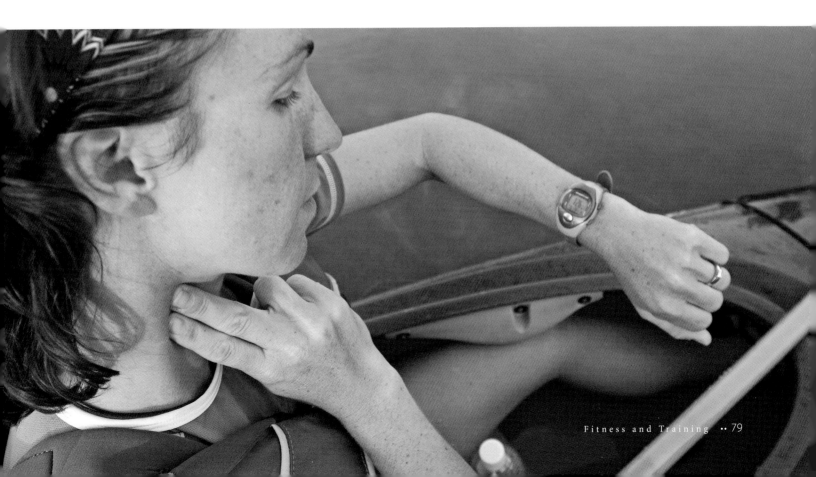

Here are three ways to roughly calculate your MHR:

Calculation Based on Averages—There are a few quick calculations that can be used to estimate or predict your MHR based on averages. Here are two to choose from, and you'll find that the results for each are very close:

$$220 - age = MHR$$
$$217 - (0.85 \times age) = MHR$$

Because your true MHR will depend on a range of factors, I recommend starting with this basic calculation to get a ballpark figure, but I recommend calculating your MHR based on actual heart rate measurements (using your heart rate monitor or one of the two methods below) when you get a chance.

Time Trial—This method can be used with any sport, including kayaking, running, biking—even cross-country skiing or snowshoeing. During the last 1–2 minutes of a time trial training session (competitive athletes) or general workout (recreational athletes), go into a full sprint. Keep checking your heart rate monitor or take your heart rate as soon as you stop and add five beats to the highest number that you get. The result should be pretty close to your MHR. There is a time trial training session set out in Week 6 of the program in this book, which is a good time to do this test and confirm your MHR.

Biggest Number—This method requires that you do a series of brief intervals where you go as hard as you can, and then use either the highest heart rate recorded on your heart rate monitor or measured immediately after you stop as your MHR. This method works well only if you have already been working out regularly. You can try this test during the Week 7 or Week 8 of the training program in this book, which includes a few interval sessions.

Zone 1

60–70% of MHR—The effort being expended in a Zone 1 workout may feel almost ridiculously easy. The temptation is often to go harder because it doesn't even feel like exercise. Don't be fooled—this type of workout is extremely important. You are training your body to burn fat as a fuel source and building a solid fitness base. This type of training is done for longer durations than other workouts so it can actually be quite fatiguing due to overall loss of energy and fluids.

Zone 2

70–75% of MHR—A Zone 2 workout is slightly more intense than a Zone 1 workout and feels more like exercise. Many people spend most of their training time in this zone. For beginner athletes, working out in this zone will deliver aerobic benefits at first, but once a base level of fitness of achieved, it is better to stay away from Zone 2 because you cease to get the optimal adaptations that you get from Zone 1 training.

Zone 3

75–80% of MHR—This zone is often referred to as race pace and is typically the fastest sustainable effort and is still aerobic exercise; Zone 4 is where you pass into anaerobic exercise. You will notice an increase in your breathing rate and may become aware of the threshold between aerobic and anaerobic types of exertion.

Zone 4

80–90% of MHR—Zone 4 requires hard effort, involves anaerobic exertion and is not sustainable. You will feel the build up of lactic acid in your muscles, which will cause them to feel tired and sluggish.

Zone 5

90–100% of MHR—At this zone you are burning your ATP—your high octane fuel source that burns out really quickly. These workouts are very hard and require you to use your aerobic and anaerobic systems and fast-twitch muscles fully. It is good to have some of these workouts scheduled at specific times in order to develop your speed. It is also important to incorporate these workouts into weeks with lower training volumes to allow your body a full recovery. As a training tool these types of sessions are great at making adaptation occur in your body, but should be planned carefully.

OTHER WAYS OF DETERMINING INTENSITY LEVELS

Here are two ways that will help you gauge what intensity level you are working out at without having to check your heart rate.

The Talk Test

The talk test is a good way to estimate how hard you are working. I've only included guidelines for Zones 1, 4 and 5 because the majority of workouts in this book are in these zones.

Zone 1—You can talk all the way through your workout and feel comfortable taking deep breaths after each sentence. If you find breathing is easy, you are probably in a low Zone 1 and could work just a little bit harder by focusing on your technique. If you like, you can occasionally check your heart rate to make sure you aren't pushing into Zone 2.

Zone 4—You can say only a few words at a time but must catch your breath before you can talk more.

Zone 5—You cannot talk and are breathing very hard.

Perceived Exertion

The harder it feels, the greater the intensity. Zone 1 training has a low perceived exertion. You should feel extremely comfortable at the pace at the beginning of this type of workout, but the longer you are out, you should feel increasingly tired. Zone 5 workouts, on the other hand, have an extremely high perceived exertion. These workouts consist of sets of short intervals of intense activity with long rest periods in between to fully recover. Zone 4 workouts are just below Zone 5, and have a medium-high level of perceived exertion.

The talk test is a good way to determine your intensity level. If you can talk comfortably, taking deep breaths after each sentence, you're in Zone 1.

Cross-Training

Because kayaking gives you a low-impact, total body workout, doing it in combination with other activities makes for terrific cross-training. Cross-training, or doing a mix of sports and activities, gives your body a break from the normal impact of training and lets your most-used muscles, tendons, bones, joints and ligaments get a brief rest or just be used in a different way, which can contribute significantly to your overall conditioning.

- **Cyclists** will benefit from kayaking by developing core and upper body strength while maintaining cardiovascular endurance. Increased strength in these areas will help with hill-climbing. Kayakers can benefit from cycling for the extra leg workouts.

- **Swimmers** and **kayakers** can apply many of the same technical principals because the reach, catch and glide are similar between the two sports. Swimming is a great complementary sport for kayakers to do if you live in an area that has an off-season, because it also helps you maintain endurance. If you get really serious about your paddling, you can even incorporate some sport-specific technical exercises with paddles by sitting on the side of the pool deck.

- **Rock climbers** will be able to keep upper body and grip strength using paddling as a way to help develop cardiovascular endurance. Kayakers will find that the strength they have developed paddling can be very enjoyably applied to climbing!

- **Runners** will benefit from the low-impact aspect of paddling because they can maintain their endurance, build upper body strength and still work the legs without any pounding for the feet and knees.

Kayaking is a fantastic complement to other fitness activities, like running or cycling. It works different your body in different ways and gives your body more chance to recover from other activities.

Nutrition

Optimal nutrition for paddling is like any other sport. It's best to establish healthy eating habits based on sound dietary practices and maintain it year-round—not just when you are training. Developing a healthy long-term eating pattern will not only help you feel better all the time, but will give you a great foundation to which you can add your workout fuel-up and recovery foods. When you eat well, you can perform longer and recover faster.

Think of your body as an engine; the more it works, the more fuel it needs. Carbohydrates provide that fuel, and it gets stored in different forms. A little high octane fuel is stored in the form of glucose in your blood, but a larger amount is stored as glycogen in your muscles. Your body can store about two hours worth of carbohydrate-supplied energy, so it must be regularly refueled by carbohydrate intake.

Depending on activity levels, the amount of carbohydrates in your diet should make up almost half of your calorie intake every day. Although most active people recognize the importance of a "high carb" diet, their diets will usually contain less than 40% carbohydrates.

Eating enough healthy carbohydrates is also important in daily recovery. In general, it's a good idea to make nutritious carbohydrate-rich foods a priority in all meals and snacks, and make sure they take the most room on your plate. The rest of your diet should consist of fresh or frozen vegetables and sources of lean protein like non-fatty cuts of beef and pork, skinless chicken, eggs and legumes like beans and lentils. Be sure to also include some healthy unsaturated fats like olive and flax seed oil. Too much fat is not good for you, but your body still needs it to function optimally. (Try adding flax seed oil to breakfast smoothies loaded with fruit and unsweetened yogurt.) A good rule to follow when choosing vegetables is to go by color: the more color, generally the more nutritious. For example, choose romaine or spinach over iceberg lettuce.

Staying hydrated means drinking about 1 quart (1 liter) per hour while exercising.

Healthy carbohydrates include things like fresh and dried fruits, root vegetables like potatoes and yams, whole grain breads and pastas, grains like rice and barley, and unsweetened cereals. When your energy requirements are high, more sugary foods can be used to add extra fuel to an already nutritious carbohydrate-rich meal, but I recommend sports drinks and energy bars over typical desserts.

Hydration

Everyone needs water to stay alive, but athletes need it to perform well. Water is vital for cooling, joint lubrication, metabolic waste removal, as well as the digestion, absorption and transport of nutrients. Dehydration is one of the biggest factors in early fatigue during exercise. Even a slight state of dehydration decreases performance, impairs cardiovascular function and if sustained for a long period of time, can lead to serious health problems.

Paddlers lose large amounts of fluid when exercising. The amount of moisture you lose through sweat depends on how hot the weather is, how long or how intensely you workout, as well as how fit you are.

It is important to drink fluids regularly throughout the day, but it is essential to drink more before you exercise. Start increasing your water intake from an hour to an hour and a half before your workout. Enough fluid should be consumed at this time so that you have clear and large volumes of urine.

In order for the rate of water intake to keep up with the rate of water loss while exercising, you should continue to increase your drinking. For some people, exercise will delay the feeling of being thirsty. I recommend that you do not rely on thirst as your first indicator. Instead, make up a simple hydration plan and stick to it. For example, you might drink between every interval or set of intervals. During long slow training days, you might set your watch to beep every 15 minutes as a reminder to drink.

Plain water is effective for replenishing fluids, but sports drinks that contain carbohydrates and electrolytes are better when you are working out. These solutions have a higher absorption rate, which allows your body to absorb more water in less time, and the carbohydrate content will provide fuel when the glycogen in your muscles is running low. These drinks also usually taste better than just plain water, and this can help encourage you to drink more and more often.

For proper hydration:

> Keep fluids readily available.

> Drink about 1 quart (1 liter) an hour when exercising, consuming it over the hour in regular intervals.

> Drink before, during and after exercise, and BEFORE you feel thirsty.

Warming Up and Stretching

Warming up is literally the process of slowly warming your muscles before you work out. The goals of the warm-up are to increase general body awareness, to improve coordination, elasticity and contractibility of muscles, and to stimulate the respiratory and cardiovascular systems. You can also use the warm-up to practice some of the less used strokes, such as the reverse stroke, sweep strokes and draw strokes. A proper warm-up should raise your body temperature by one or two degrees Celsius and is divided into three phases: general warm-up, stretching, and a sport-specific activity. The whole thing should take about 10–15 minutes.

GENERAL WARM-UP

The general warm-up should begin with joint rotations, starting with your feet and working your way up. Perform slow circular movements, both clockwise and counter-clockwise, until the joints seem to move smoothly. Next, do a few minutes of light aerobic activity to start slightly elevating your heart rate. A short light jog or bike ride works well.

STRETCHING

Make sure that you are well warmed up before you begin some light stretching. It is not a good idea to attempt to stretch before your muscles are warm. Once warm, they are more elastic and supple and ready for some slow, relaxed stretching. Start with your back and other large muscle groups. Work your upper body and lower body systematically from larger muscles to smaller muscles. Stretching before a workout loosens stiff muscles and gets the muscles ready to work; it is not the time to try to increase your flexibility. Stretch to increase flexibility during your cool-down.

If you are really short of time, try to at least stretch all the muscles that will be heavily used during your workout. You can even do some stretches in your boat.

WARMING UP IN YOUR BOAT

Devote the last part of your warm-up to performing the same movements that will be used during the training session, but at a reduced intensity. So if you are about to do speed work, you should paddle fairly fast in the warm-up; if you are about to do a long slow distance workout, you can do much more relaxed paddling. Remember, you are just trying to get your body ready for the workout ahead by improving coordination, balance, strength and response time.

As mentioned before, the warm-up is also a great time to practice some of the less used strokes and focus on developing good technique. Start by taking 25 reverse strokes, and then use a combination of forward sweeps and reverse sweeps to pivot your boat in circles while sitting still on the water. To spin your boat to the left, use a forward sweep on the right followed by a reverse sweep on the left. After two full circles, spin the other way using a forward sweep on the left and reverse sweep on the right. To end your warm-up, take 10 draw strokes on each side of your boat.

Your warm-up should leave you feeling ready to work out both physically and mentally. When done properly, it will help improve your performance; but an improper warm-up, or no warm-up at all, can greatly increase your risk of injury.

Cooling Down

A good cool-down will reduce muscle fatigue and soreness, especially if you have produced a lot of lactic acid during your workout. The cool-down should be sport-specific, so for example, if you have been running, your cool-down will involve a light jog or brisk walk; for kayaking it will be some light paddling. Take between 5 and 20 minutes to cool-down, reduce your intensity and allow your heart rate to come down.

One way to ensure a good cool-down is to end your kayaking workout about half a mile (or a kilometer) away from the take-out or end point, which will give your body the opportunity to recover as you paddle back more slowly. Like the warm-up, the cool-down is a great time to work on technique. Try mentally focusing on your balance, coordination, timing or whatever you feel needs a little work. I also begin some light stretching as I am putting the boat away.

Increasing Flexibility

Always save some time at the end of your workout for some relaxed stretching so that you can develop flexibility and allow yourself to transition smoothly into the rest of your day. A proper cool-down followed by stretching can reduce cramping, tightening and soreness in fatigued muscles and will make you feel better and recover faster.

Try to isolate specific muscles with each stretch you perform. The fewer muscles you try to stretch at once, the better. For example, stretch one hamstring at a time rather than both at once. By isolating the muscle you are stretching, you experience resistance from fewer muscle groups, which gives you greater control over the stretch and allows you to more easily adjust the intensity. Work each stretch for at least 20 seconds, and up to a full minute or more.

Proper breathing relaxes the body and allows you to go deeper into your stretches. Inhale slowly through your nose, expand your entire abdomen (not just your ribcage), hold your breath a moment and then exhale slowly through your nose or mouth. Do not force your breaths, but naturally allow your abdomen to draw and expel air. Don't force positions that hurt; increase your flexibility gradually. Stretching should be a relaxing reward at the end of a good workout. Never bounce in a stretch.

Stretching should be a relaxing reward at the end of a good workout. Never bounce in a stretch.

To stretch the side of your shoulder and the back of your upper arm:

1. While sitting or standing, place your right hand on your left shoulder.

2. With your left hand, pull your right elbow across your chest and toward your left shoulder. Hold it there for 20 seconds.

3. Repeat on the other side.

To stretch your chest and shoulders:

1. While sitting or standing, grab your paddle at both ends where the shaft meets the blade.

2. Lift the paddle over and behind your head until you feel a light stretch. Hold it there for 20 seconds.

To stretch your lower back, hips and neck:

1. Sit on the floor with your left leg straight out in front you.

2. Cross your right foot over your left leg and place it just outside of your left knee.

3. Bend your left elbow and rest it on the outside of your right knee.

4. Place your right hand behind your right hip on the ground.

5. Rotate your head and upper body to the right and look over your right shoulder.

6. Hold the position for 20 seconds.

7. Repeat on the other side.

To stretch your hamstrings:

1. While standing up, cross your left leg in front of your right leg and place your left foot just beside your right foot.

2. Bending at the hips, bring your chest towards your left thigh.

3. Let the weight of your head and arms drop to help pull your upper body downward. If you feel pressure on your back, bend both legs slightly.

4. Hold the position for 20 seconds.

5. Repeat on the other side.

CHAPTER 6:

8-Week Program

> Program Overview

> Week 1 to 4: Stamina and
General Fitness

> Week 5 to 8: Strength and
Endurance Development

Program Overview

In the pages that follow, I present my 8-week program for kayaking fitness, designed to give you maximum benefits in a limited timeframe, and targeted for three different levels: beginner, intermediate and advanced. A different time, in minutes, is provided for each level and for each workout. By using heart rate zones as a guide, this program allows anyone of any fitness level to work within their personal limits. Fit these workouts into your week and you will strengthen your heart and lungs, and tone muscles throughout your body. For more information about calculating your personal heart rate zones, see the section on *Heart Rate Zones* in Chapter 5.

Some of the workouts are challenging, but they are also varied and fun—sure to address all aspects of training: strength, endurance, technique and speed. The program is designed to include **four workouts a week,** with rest days for your body to adapt and recover. If you are a more casual paddler, you can also use the program as a guideline and adapt it to suit your needs. However, I strongly encourage paddlers of every level to give the whole program a try. Make the time. Commit to it. Among the tremendous benefits of regular training are more energy, vitality and a more positive mental outlook, which all provide you with a better overall quality of life.

TIP

Finding a workout partner who is starting at about the same level as you and keen to do the program too can make every session more fun and help you both feel more committed to exercising regularly. You can encourage each other, observe and correct each others' technique, groan together about the harder workouts, and generally share in the enjoyment of getting more fit!

I have split up the training into two, easy-to-follow, 4-week sections:

Weeks 1 to 4: Stamina and General Fitness

Weeks 5 to 8: Strength and Endurance

The first four weeks are designed to be a capacity builder that will have you working out at a lower heart rate. The workouts get more intense in the second four weeks, with generally higher heart rate targets.

DETERMINING YOUR FITNESS LEVEL

Beginner—If you engage in low-intensity physical activity once a week or less, choose the beginner workout durations. Couch potatoes are welcome in this category too!

Intermediate—You engage in physical activity semi-regularly, at least once or twice a week, but have never or don't usually follow training schedules. You may also be sporadic in your level of activity, doing nothing for a few weeks and alternating with periods of more regular exercising.

Advanced—You are already in good shape, exercise three or more times a week, and are looking for a training program that will advance your fitness to the next level.

Try your best to do all workouts in the boat. If you must, you can use running, swimming or cycling to substitute for a workout. For off-season or bad-weather training, consider workouts on an indoor kayaking ergometer (often called an "erg"). The erg is to a kayaker what a treadmill is to a runner. If you can't find a kayaking ergometer, most indoor gyms are equipped with rowing ergs which will at least work many of the same muscle groups.

Core strength exercises like push-ups, sit-ups, pull-ups and dips, yoga and Pilates can also complement this paddling program well.

Heart Rate Zones— Quick Summary

Remember to stick to the prescribed zones for each workout. People often go either too hard or too easy to reap any benefits, or even worse, end up doing damage. Here's a quick refresher on the zones:

Zone 1: (60–70% of MHR) Frequently used in this program, this is your long distance, steady and easy intensity zone. You can talk comfortably, but still need to take good breaths between each sentence.

Zone 2: (70–75% of MHR) Slightly more intense than Zone 1. You will very rarely work in this zone.

Zone 3: (75–80% of MHR) A good pace for racing. This is also known as your anaerobic threshold because you will be working hard enough to just reach the point where you are about to switch from aerobic to anaerobic. This means that you will only be able to say a few words before you need another breath and will be working very hard.

Zone 4: (80–90% of MHR) Requires hard effort, which is not sustainable. The anaerobic lactic system is at work in Zone 4. Your muscles will feel the build up of lactic acid, which will cause them to feel sluggish.

Zone 5: (90–100% of MHR) This is your highest intensity possible, using quick-burning fuel and resulting in a lactic acid burn in your muscles. You will not be able to talk. You will only ever work at this zone in short spurts and should give yourself ample recovery time.

Your fitness level will determine which of the programs will best suit your needs.

Week 1 to 4: Stamina and General Fitness

Over the first four weeks, you will develop the muscle groups specific to kayaking, paddling technique and a stronger fitness base. This period will prepare you for the strength and endurance workouts of the last four weeks.

These first four weeks are characterized by a few intensity drills, several longer paddling sessions in a steady aerobic zone and sessions that will allow you to focus on your skills.

Week 1: Overview

WEEK 1	DAY 1	DAY 2	DAY 3	DAY 4
Name of Workout	Posture Perfect	Picking up the Pace	Junk Paddle	Easy Flow
Intensity Level	Easy Zone 1	Easy and intense Zone 1 and 3–4	Easy Zone 1 and 2	Easy Zone 1
Duration	Beginner: 45 min Intermediate: 55 min Advanced: 65 min	Beginner: 40 min Intermediate: 50 min Advanced: 60 min	Beginner: 50 min Intermediate: 60 min Advanced: 70 min	Beginner: 60 min Intermediate: 75 min Advanced: 90 min

Week 1 **Day 1**

Name of Workout:	**POSTURE PERFECT**	
Type:	Skills and Rhythm	
Intensity Level:	Easy, Zone 1	
Duration:	Warm-up	10 min
	Workout	Beginner—25 min
		Intermediate—35 min
		Advanced—45 min
	Cool-down	10 min

INSTRUCTIONS:

The goal is to get on the water and start paddling. Focus less on how long or hard you are paddling, and more on skills and technique. Day 1 workouts throughout the program will focus on technical aspects more than intensity. So just go out and have an easy paddle, maintaining Zone 1 levels of exertion. During this session, focus on paddling with good posture. This means sitting up straight with a slight forward lean in the upper body and your legs bent.

As you spend more time in a kayak and your skills improve, your paddle will start to feel like a natural extension of your arms. When holding your paddle, maintain a secure but light grip on it. An overly tight grip will only lead to sore forearms and potential tendonitis.

Good paddling posture will give you the most control over your boat's edging, let you rotate your upper body the most effectively, and give your strokes the most power.

Week 1 **Day 2**

Name of Workout:	**PICKING UP THE PACE**	
Type:	Interval	
Intensity Level:	Easy (Zone 1) with bursts of more intense (Zone 3–4)	
Duration:	Warm-up	10 min
	Workout	Beginner—20 min
		Intermediate—30 min
		Advanced—40 min
	Cool-down	10 min

INSTRUCTIONS:

This session introduces you to intensity training, but without too much structure or formality. The goal of this and other threshold workouts is to prepare your body and mind for more intense exertion in the future. In other words, this workout is designed to help you get more familiar with different levels of power and to learn to push your limits.

Warm-up is easy and you are encouraged to practice good padding technique.

To start the workout, begin to pick up the pace for around 5 minutes. Vary your higher level of intensity until you feel you have reached Zone 4. Notice how this feels in your body, but don't push it too long or hard. Paddle at an easier pace until your heart rate is back down to Zone 1. Continue with easy paddling for 5–10 more minutes until you feel ready for another 5-minute challenge of higher intensity paddling. By the end of the workout you should have completed between three and six of these high intensity bursts.

These 5-minute intervals will start building your overall cardiovascular fitness and help get you mentally prepared for higher exertion activities.

The talk test is a good gauge for when your heart rate has reached Zone 4. When you've reached Zone 4, you'll only be able to say a few words at a time, and will need to catch your breath before you can talk more.

Week 1 **Day 3**

Name of Workout:	**JUNK PADDLE**	
Type:	Recovery	
Intensity Level:	Easy, Zone 1	
Duration:	Warm-up	10 min
	Workout	Beginner—30 min
		Intermediate—40 min
		Advanced—50 min
	Cool-down	10 min

INSTRUCTIONS:

This workout is called a "junk paddle" because I don't want you to think of it as training. Just go out for a fun paddle, and don't focus too hard on what zone you are in or what distance you are travelling. You are in recovery mode from the last, more strenuous workout, and are now out to build your body's aerobic system and sport-specific muscles.

The whole workout is intended to be done in Zone 1, (so you should be able to carry on a conversation the entire time), but you can go higher or lower, as long as you are enjoying yourself.

Throw in three sets of relaxed, 1-minute long sets of back paddling to mix things up and get different muscles involved. While doing so, concentrate on using full body rotation for your back strokes.

A "junk paddle" refers to a paddle in which you're just out there having a good time, keeping your heart rate in Zone 1.

The junk paddle is a great time to practice some of your other strokes. When practicing your back strokes, focus on rotating your body aggressively during the wind-up phase of the stroke.

Week 1 **Day 4**

Name of Workout:	**EASY FLOW**	
Type:	Long, slow distance	
Intensity Level:	Easy, Zone 1	
Duration:	Warm-up	10 min
	Workout	Beginner—40 min
		Intermediate—55 min
		Advanced—70 min
	Cool-down	10 min

INSTRUCTIONS:

The goal of this session is to build a paddling fitness base and get your muscles accustomed to long training sessions in the boat. These workouts are ideal for overall conditioning and fat burning. The key is economy of effort. Stay relaxed in the boat, paddle efficiently and keep hydrated. Intersperse the workout with three 1-minute sets of back paddling to help strengthen other muscles.

An "Easy Flow" workout is similar to the junk paddle in intensity, but you'll put more effort into maintaining a smooth paddling cadence and using proper technique.

Week 2: **Overview**

WEEK 1	DAY 1	DAY 2	DAY 3	DAY 4
Name of Workout	Straight-Arm Paddling	Pacemaker	Junk Paddle	LSD Trip
Intensity Level	Easy Zone 1	Easy and intense Zone 1 and 4	Easy Zone 1 and 2	Easy Zone 1
Duration	Beginner: 50 min Intermediate: 60 min Advanced: 70 min	Beginner: 50 min Intermediate: 60 min Advanced: 70 min	Beginner: 55 min Intermediate: 65 min Advanced: 75 min	Beginner: 65 min Intermediate: 80 min Advanced: 95 min

Week 2 **Day 1**

Name of Workout:	STRAIGHT-ARM PADDLING	
Type:	Skills	
Intensity Level:	Easy, Zone 1	
Duration:	Warm-up	10 min with 1 min of back paddling
	Workout	Beginner—30 min
		Intermediate—40 min
		Advanced—50 min
	Cool-down	10 min with 1 min of back paddling

INSTRUCTIONS:
Like the very first workout, the goal is to get on the water and paddle at a consistent, easy pace. Time is not as important as practicing skills and technique and developing a rhythm. For this entire workout, focus on using your core muscles to generate the torso rotation for the strength and power of the stroke. To help you develop your torso rotation, try the Straight-Arm Paddling drill during your warm-up and cool-down, and perform two 1-minute sets of the drill during your workout.

STRAIGHT-ARM PADDLING DRILL
By paddling with your arms locked at the elbows, you won't be able to pull on your paddle with your arms, which means that you'll be forced to use the power of torso rotation for your strokes. Think of your whole upper body as a single unit that must work as one to pull the paddle through the water.

Week 2 **Day 2**

Name of Workout:	**PACEMAKER**	
Type:	Intervals	
Intensity Level:	Easy, Zone 1 with bursts of higher intensity Zone 4	
Duration:	Warm-up	10 min
	Workout	Beginner—30 min or 3 sets
		Intermediate—40 min or 4 sets
		Advanced—50 min or 5 sets
	Cool-down	10 min

INSTRUCTIONS:

This session introduces you to more structured intensity training. Go 5 minutes at a high Zone 3 or low Zone 4, and then 5 minutes at a Zone 1, easy paddle. High Zone 3 or Low Zone 4 is often referred to as "race pace" because it is the level of exertion you would use for a short race (going hard, but able to sustain yourself at this level for half an hour or more).

Repeat each 10-minute cycle for the duration of your workout.

Work hard enough that by the end you feel as though you could not do another set. If you start to get tired, bored or feel your muscles going lactic during one of the intervals, develop mental toughness by getting through the workout. (It can help to think of a positive or silly or meaningful phrase to repeat to yourself as you do it.) Your muscular fatigue is a positive sign of a body in training. These exercises will get easier and more

A tandem kayak can be a great fitness tool, but to really work well, you and your partner should have similar goals and expectations. As a general rule, the stronger paddler should in the stern of the boat and be responsible for steering. The bow paddler can then take breaks while the stern paddler continues with their workout.

It is most efficient to paddle a tandem kayak in unison. The front paddler establishes the pace and the stern paddler keeps in time with it.

comfortable as you get used to this feeling, and as you find yourself reaping the benefits of this hard work. Of course, listen to your body and pay attention if you think you are causing a strain or tear on a muscle or ligament—fight through fatigue and muscular ache, but do not push it if you feel any sharp pain or suspect that you are injuring yourself. With proper hydration, warm-up and cool-down, these intervals should be a good challenge, but not damaging in any way.

Week 2 **Day 3**

Name of Workout:	JUNK PADDLE	
Type:	Recovery	
Intensity Level:	Easy, Zone 1	
Duration:	Warm-up	10 min
	Workout	Beginner—35 min
		Intermediate—45 min
		Advanced—55 min
	Cool-down	10 min

INSTRUCTIONS:

This workout is designed with recovery in mind. Take the time to review your paddling skills and technique at a relaxed pace. Remember: Zone 1 means no heavy breathing. Tinker around a familiar paddling spot or go explore a new area. Try paddling backwards or try maneuvering the kayak around obstacles. Try practicing holding the boat on each edge as you paddle forward, which will help you develop your core strength, your balance and your overall comfort in the kayak.

Week 2 **Day 4**

Name of Workout:	**LSD TRIP**	
Type:	Long slow distance	
Intensity Level:	Easy, Zone 1	
Duration:	Warm-up	10 min
	Workout	Beginner—45 min
		Intermediate—60 min
		Advanced—75 min
	Cool-down	10 min

INSTRUCTIONS:

Each week we will do one long slow distance (LSD) Zone 1 workout, increasing in duration each time. Go easy, but remain focused on your technique. LSD workouts are a good time to enjoy the scenery so choose a trip or location that will sustain your interest. River trips are a good option because you have current, an ever-changing landscape and a potential adventure. To continue to develop your all-around paddling skills, incorporate four 1-minute sets of back paddling into this session.

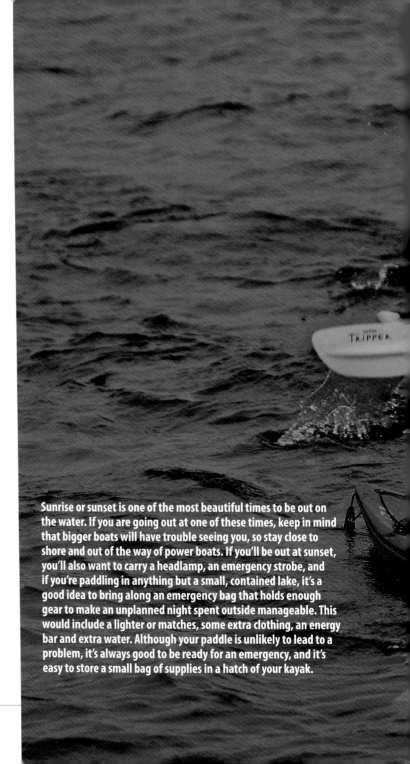

Sunrise or sunset is one of the most beautiful times to be out on the water. If you are going out at one of these times, keep in mind that bigger boats will have trouble seeing you, so stay close to shore and out of the way of power boats. If you'll be out at sunset, you'll also want to carry a headlamp, an emergency strobe, and if you're paddling in anything but a small, contained lake, it's a good idea to bring along an emergency bag that holds enough gear to make an unplanned night spent outside manageable. This would include a lighter or matches, some extra clothing, an energy bar and extra water. Although your paddle is unlikely to lead to a problem, it's always good to be ready for an emergency, and it's easy to store a small bag of supplies in a hatch of your kayak.

Week 3: **Overview**

WEEK 1	DAY 1	DAY 2	DAY 3	DAY 4
Name of Workout	Pause N' Stroke	Swedish for Speed-Play	Junk Paddle	LSD Trip
Intensity Level	Easy Zone 1	Easy and intense Zone 1 and 4	Easy Zone 1 and 2	Easy Zone 1
Duration	Beginner: 60 min Intermediate: 70 min Advanced: 80 min	Beginner: 45 min Intermediate: 43 min Advanced: 43 min	Beginner: 55 min Intermediate: 65 min Advanced: 75 min	Beginner: 80 min Intermediate: 100 min Advanced: 120 min

Week 3 **Day 1**

Name of Workout:	**PAUSE N' STROKE**	
Type:	Skills	
Intensity Level:	Easy, Zone 1	
Duration:	Warm-up	10 min with sweeps and draw strokes in each direction
	Workout	Beginner—40 min
		Intermediate—50 min
		Advanced—60 min
	Cool-down	10 min with some light back paddling

INSTRUCTIONS:
The Pause N' Stroke drill is designed to improve your focus while padding. This is not a heavy workout—you should remain at a constant, easy, Zone 1 intensity. After your warm-up, alternate between 5 minutes of practicing the drill with 15 minutes of easy paddling.

PAUSE N' STROKE DRILL
This drill is designed to improve the catch phase of your forward stroke. It involves pausing slightly as you bring your paddle down towards the water for the catch. This pause should happen just before you start pushing the paddle down and into the water. While pausing, think about extending your bottom hand and winding up your upper body to get a full extension. With the bottom arm and shoulder fully extended, push the paddle shaft down with the top hand and engage the fully-submerged blade in the water early in the stroke.

Week 3 **Day 2**

Name of Workout:	**SWEDISH FOR SPEED-PLAY**	
Type:	Intervals	
Intensity Level:	Easy, Zone 1 with intervals of high intensity, upper Zone 4	
Duration:	Warm-up	10 min, including 1 min of back paddling
	Workout	Beginner— 25 min total 2 min hard, 4 min easy 2 min hard, 4 min easy 4 min hard, 4 min easy 2 min hard, 2 min easy 1 min hard
		Intermediate— 23 min total 2 min hard, 2 min easy 4 min hard, 4 min easy 4 min hard, 2 min easy 2 min hard, 2 min easy 1 min hard
		Advanced— 23 min total 2 min hard, 2 min easy 3 min hard, 3 min easy 5 min hard, 3 min easy 3 min hard, 1 min easy 1 min hard
	Cool-down	10 min, (include some back paddling as part of the cool down)

INSTRUCTIONS:

This workout involves doing "fartleks"— a funny-sounding word in English that is Swedish for "speed-play". These exercises are designed to improve your higher levels of physical exertion as well as to develop your mental game. You are looking to discover a new higher gear during this workout.

These are your first real intervals, so you will be alternating between Zone 4 bursts of going hard and Zone 1 periods of recovery, following a regimented pattern. During the intervals, you will bring yourself right up to Zone 4 as quickly as possible and hold it there for the duration, going right to the brink of your anaerobic threshold. It won't necessarily feel good in the moment, but you will feel great once you are done. Fartleks will also bring you significant fitness benefits, so it's worth a few minutes of discomfort. You can do it!

You will go as hard as you can go for the period of intensity. Recovery will be slow and easy paddling to bring your heart rate down, but do not stop all activity.

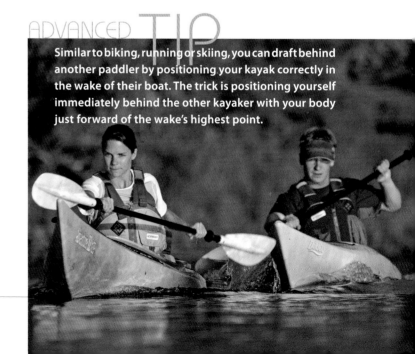

ADVANCED TIP

Similar to biking, running or skiing, you can draft behind another paddler by positioning your kayak correctly in the wake of their boat. The trick is positioning yourself immediately behind the other kayaker with your body just forward of the wake's highest point.

Week 3 **Day 3**

Name of Workout:	**JUNK PADDLE**	
Type:	Recovery	
Intensity Level:	Easy, Zone 1	
Duration:	Warm-up	10 min with sweeps and draw strokes in each direction
	Workout	Beginner—35 min
		Intermediate—45 min
		Advanced—55 min
	Cool-down	10 min

INSTRUCTIONS:

You will probably be tired from your last workout. Even if you are sore or lethargic, it is good to get out on the water and "spin the paddle". Completing this gentle Zone 1 workout will actually speed recovery and adaptation.

Still not sure if you're going at an easy enough pace? Remember: you should be able to carry on a conversation with the person paddling next to you. At some point during this session, switch it up and back paddle for a single 1-minute interval, just to stimulate the opposing muscle groups.

One of the greatest things about kayaks is how they can get you to unique places. An easier workout follows every harder one, and these recovery sessions are great for scenic locations because your focus should be on relaxing and enjoying yourself.

Week 3 **Day 4**

Name of Workout:	**LSD TRIP**	
Type:	Long slow distance	
Intensity Level:	Easy, Zone 1	
Duration:	Warm-up	10 min, including 1 minute of back paddling
	Workout	Beginner—60 min
		Intermediate—80 min
		Advanced—100 min
	Cool-down	10 min

INSTRUCTIONS:

Similar to your LSD paddle last week, the goal today is to continue building your paddling fitness base and get your muscles accustomed to long sessions in the boat. Work the opposite muscle groups by back paddling for short periods. These workouts are ideal for overall conditioning and fat burning. The key is economy of effort. Stay relaxed in the boat, paddle efficiently and keep hydrated.

Sea kayaks are between 16 and 18 feet in length and narrower than recreational kayaks. This makes them less stable but significantly faster than recreational boats. There is a common misconception that sea kayaks are only designed for paddling in the open ocean, but that couldn't be further from the truth. Sea kayaks are great boats for any type of water. The only condition for using a sea kayak is that you are comfortable knowing that there is a better chance of flipping, and that due to the smaller cockpit, wet exiting will take you a second or two longer.

Week 4: **Overview**

WEEK 1	DAY 1	DAY 2	DAY 3	DAY 4
Name of Workout	Leg Press	True Intervals	Junk Paddle	LSD Trip
Intensity Level	Easy Zone 1	Easy and intense Zone 1 and 4	Easy Zone 1 and 2	Easy Zone 1
Duration	Beginner: 60 min Intermediate: 70 min Advanced: 80 min	Beginner: 50 min Intermediate: 60 min Advanced: 70 min	Beginner: 65 min Intermediate: 75 min Advanced: 85 min	Beginner: 100 min Intermediate: 120 min Advanced: 140 min

Week 4 **Day 1**

Name of Workout:	**LEG PRESS**	
Type:	Skills and Rhythm	
Intensity Level:	Easy, Zone 1	
Duration:	Warm-up	10 min, with sweeps and draw strokes in each direction
	Workout	Beginner—40 min
		Intermediate—50 min
		Advanced—60 min
	Cool-down	10 min

INSTRUCTIONS:

Just like all other Day 1 workouts, focus on technique rather than distance or intensity. This is not a heavy workout—remain at a constant, easy pace. After you warm-up, alternate between 5 minutes of practicing the Leg Press drill with 15 minutes of easy paddling.

The technique focus of today's drill is on using the power in your legs with each stroke. Try today's drill for 1 minute while back paddling to help develop your timing and coordination. When back paddling, you'll push and straighten the leg that on the opposite side of your active paddle blade.

LEG PRESS DRILL

During the catch phase of the forward stroke, start applying pressure on the foot peg with the leg that is on the same side as your active paddle blade. As you pull on your paddle, continue to push aggressively on the foot peg so that by the time your stroke has finished, your leg is fully extended. You can also think of pushing your knee toward the bottom of the boat as you take your stroke. This motion helps you maximize your torso rotation because it forces your body to unwind fully.

Week 4 **Day 2**

Name of Workout:	TRUE INTERVALS	
Type:	Intervals	
Intensity Level:	Easy, Zone 1 with hard, Zone 4	
Duration:	Warm-up	10 min, including 1 minute of back paddling
	Workout	Beginner—30 min total 7 min hard, 3 min easy (three times total)
		Intermediate—40 min total 7 min hard, 3 min easy (four times total)
		Advanced—50 min total 7 min hard, 3 min easy (five times total)
	Cool-down	10 min

INSTRUCTIONS:

Focus on pushing to your maximum today during the hard phase of these intervals, and then really relaxing and going slow for the recovery phase.

Advanced paddlers—record or pay attention to your distance for each 7-minute hard paddle to evaluate whether you are remaining consistent in your efforts. A GPS is a good tool for this, or you can paddle the same stretch of water for each interval.

Plastic or fibreglass paddles flex a lot more than those made of carbon fibre or Kevlar. This flex acts as a cushion for your joints—but sacrifices power.

Thanks to the slow shutter speed of this photo, you can clearly see how little the top hand punches during the forward stroke.

Week 4 **Day 3**

Name of Workout:	JUNK PADDLE	
Type:	Recovery	
Intensity Level:	Easy, Zone 1	
Duration:	Warm-up	10 min, with sweeps and draw strokes in each direction
	Workout	Beginner—45 min
		Intermediate—55 min
		Advanced—65 min
	Cool-down	10 min

INSTRUCTIONS:

Keeping your exertion level constant and easy, we will now start to add time and distance to these workouts. Nothing has changed for these "junk paddles" except the amount of time spent in the boat. Take a moment to do two 1-minute back paddling sets and then paddle a minute each with your boat on one edge and then the other.

For recreational kayaks with high back bands, there are PFDs available that don't have any flotation in the lower back. This particular kayak has a large cockpit with a coaming that would allow the paddler to use a skirt, but in such calm, warm conditions, there really isn't any need for one.

Week 4 **Day 4**

Name of Workout:	**LSD TRIP**	
Type:	Recovery	
Intensity Level:	Easy, Zone 1	
Duration:	Warm-up	10 min, including 1 minute of back paddling
	Workout	Beginner—80 min
		Intermediate—100 min
		Advanced—120 min
	Cool-down	10 min

INSTRUCTIONS:

This stamina-boosting session is designed to increase your endurance. As we add more time to these long, slow paddles, remember to keep your heart rate in Zone 1. The workout will feel harder toward the end simply because it requires a longer time in the boat.

If you would like to paddle along a shoreline that doesn't provide you with the option of simply swimming to shore and walking home should a boat capsize, your group needs to be well practiced and confident with kayak rescue techniques.

Week 5 to 8:
Strength and Endurance Development

The goal of this last cycle is to make further improvements to your paddling strength and get more kayak-specific endurance. You should be in the boat for as many of the workouts as you can during this cycle. You will be working harder, so get ready for it! The long Day 4 paddles will get longer, and the short interval workouts will get gradually more intense. Workouts will be more clearly defined and structured. Building on the first four weeks, we will do intense interval sessions at least once a week and long steady distance paddling on the other days. Sprint workouts will also be introduced, where you will be working as hard as possible and experiencing some discomfort from lactic build-up in muscles. By the end of Week 8, you will be in top shape!

Week 5: **Overview**

WEEK 1	DAY 1	DAY 2	DAY 3	DAY 4
Name of Workout	Velcro Forehead	Pyramids	Junk Paddle	LSD Trip
Intensity Level	Easy and intense Zone 1 and 3 or 4	Easy and intense Zone 1 and 4	Easy Zone 1 and 2	Easy Zone 1
Duration	Beginner: 50 min Intermediate: 75 min Advanced: 85 min	Beginner: 56 min Intermediate: 74 min Advanced: 92 min	Beginner: 75 min Intermediate: 85 min Advanced: 95 min	Beginner: 110 min Intermediate: 130 min Advanced: 150 min

Week 5 **Day 1**

Name of Workout:	**VELCRO FOREHEAD**	
Type:	Easy, Zone 1 alternating with higher intensity, Zone 3 or 4	
Intensity Level:	Easy, Zone 1	
Duration:	Warm-up	10 min, with 2 min of Velcro Forehead Drill
	Workout	Beginner—50 min
		Intermediate—65 min
		Advanced—75 min
	All levels: 15 min harder, 10 min easy with 1 min drill	
	Cool-down	10 min

INSTRUCTIONS:

Unlike Day 1 workouts of the first four weeks, we are now going to introduce some intensity paddling to the skill and technique practice. The primary focus is still on technique and the intensity is at an easier intensity than the interval sessions. Because you will be going hard for 15 minutes at a time, you have to set a pace for yourself that you can sustain for the entire duration. As mentioned earlier, this is your "race pace" or the fastest you can go for a long time.

Practice the Velcro Forehead Drill during the warm-up, and for 1 minute during the 10 minute easy paddling periods.

VELCRO FOREHEAD DRILL

This drill is designed to promote the use of torso rotation and to limit the punching action of the top hand during the foreword stroke. The end result will be a more powerful and efficient forward stroke.

To do the Velcro Forehead drill, place the back of your top hand against your forehead before the catch phase of your forward stroke, and then leave it there for the duration of the stroke.

Week 5 **Day 2**

Name of Workout:	**PYRAMIDS**	
Type:	Intervals	
Intensity Level:	Easy, Zone 1 with intervals of hard Zone 4	
Duration:	Warm-up	10 min, with 1 minute of back paddling
	Workout	1 min hard, 1 min easy 2 min hard, 1 min easy 3 min hard, 1 min easy 3 min hard, 1 min easy 2 min hard, 1 min easy 1 min hard, 1 min easy
		Beginner—36 min Do this workout 2 times
		Intermediate—54 min Do this workout 3 times
		Advanced—72 min Do this workout 4 times
	Cool-down	10 min or longer

INSTRUCTIONS:

Focus on pushing to your absolute maximum level of performance today. Pyramids are a combination of all the different kinds of intervals you have done so far in this program. It combines the best elements of interval training into one effective and complete workout. As usual, the hard portion of the cycle is done at your maximum intensity and the "easy" portion is at a low Zone 1 intensity.

During hard paddling sessions, remember to drink plenty of water and give yourself sufficient cool-down time to help flush the lactic acid from your muscles.

Week 5 **Day 3**

Name of Workout:	JUNK PADDLE	
Type:	Recovery	
Intensity Level:	Easy, Zone 1	
Duration:	Warm-up	10 min, with sweeps and draw strokes in each direction
	Workout	Beginner—55 min
		Intermediate—65 min
		Advanced—75 min
	Cool-down	10 min

INSTRUCTIONS:

This is your well-earned recovery paddle. You may feel tired today, but getting out and paddling through this workout will help your body assimilate all the work it has been doing in the previous workouts. Keep your exertion level constant and easy. Nothing has changed for these "junk paddles" except that the amount of time spent in the boat is still slightly increasing. Intersperse your regular forward paddling with some edging and back paddling to stimulate supportive muscle groups.

The ideal stroke is "quiet", meaning it has minimal splash. Take a few moments during today's junk paddle and focus on performing a stroke that carries you silently through the water. One of the tricks to doing this is to ensure that your blade is completely submerged in the water during the catch phase before you pull on it.

Week 5 **Day 4**

Name of Workout:	**LSD TRIP**	
Type:	Long slow distance	
Intensity Level:	Easy, Zone 1	
Duration:	Warm-up	10 min, with 1 min back paddling
	Workout	Beginner—90 min
		Intermediate—110 min
		Advanced—130 min
	Cool-down	10 min

INSTRUCTIONS:

This workout will help increase your endurance. As we add more time to these long, slow paddles, remember to keep your heart rate low. These longer training sessions might start to feel more mentally challenging because you will be paddling for longer durations. The trick here is to make it fun. Choose a new route or a turn-around point that's just a little further than you went last time so that you won't always be looking at your watch. For variety and to balance out the development of your muscle groups, don't forget to throw a few minutes of back paddling into the session too.

Week 6: **Overview**

WEEK 1	DAY 1	DAY 2	DAY 3	DAY 4
Name of Workout	Butt Walk	Time Trial	Junk Paddle	LSD Trip
Intensity Level	Easy and intense Zone 1 and 3 or 4	Intense Zone 3 or 4	Easy Zone 1 and 2	Easy Zone 1
Duration	Beginner: 68 min Intermediate: 80 min Advanced: 92 min	Beginner: 4000 m Intermediate: 6000 m Advanced: 8000 m	Beginner: 85 min Intermediate: 95 min Advanced: 105 min	Beginner: 120 min Intermediate: 140 min Advanced: 160 min

Week 6 **Day 1**

Name of Workout:	**BUTT WALK**	
Type:	Skills and Rhythm	
Intensity Level:	Easy, Zone 1 alternating with hard, Zone 3 or 4	
Duration:	Warm-up	10 min, with 2 minutes of drill
	Workout	Beginner—48 min
		Intermediate—60 min
		Advanced—72 min
	All levels—alternate 6 min hard, 6 min easy with 1 min drill	
	Cool-down	10 min

INSTRUCTIONS:

Similar to last week, we will continue with some intensity paddling along with skill and technique practice. Alternate 6 minutes hard with 6 minutes easy. When you go hard, work at a race pace (Zone 3) or low Zone 4 intensity. When you are doing the easy phase, include 1 minute of the Butt Walk drill. All this hard work will really help increase your stamina and give you more energy.

BUTT WALK DRILL

The purpose of this drill is to help you understand how your hips and butt are involved in your strokes. Think of your body as a single unit that must work as one to pull the paddle through the water. As you extend one arm forward to initiate a stroke, your hips should also be slightly rotated on the seat toward that side. It should feel as though the butt cheek on that side has moved forward on the seat. In this drill, focus on sliding each butt cheek forward for every stroke. It will help to use a pause stroke (see Week 3, Day 1) while practicing this so that you have more time to shift your hips. You can also do this drill while back paddling, although it will be the butt cheek on the opposite side of the active blade that slides forward.

Week 6 **Day 2**

Name of Workout:	**TIME TRIAL**	
Type:	Race Pace	
Intensity Level:	Hard, Zone 3 or 4	
Duration:	Warm-up	10 min, with sweeps and draw strokes in each direction
	Workout	Beginner—4000 yards or meters, once
		Intermediate—3000 yards or meters twice, or 6000 yards or meters once
		Advanced—4000 yards or meters twice, or 8000 yards or meters once
	Cool-down	10 min or longer

INSTRUCTIONS:

A time trial allows you to see how fast you can travel a certain distance. It is a great way to measure your fitness level and test yourself. Use a GPS or a pre-measured distance and record your time over the indicated distance. Keep this for your records, as it will be very useful to compare your results to time trial workouts in the future. Get out there and remember to have fun!

Make sure to begin any time trial day with a thorough warm-up and drink plenty of fluids.

For a good aggressive forward stroke, your top hand should stay around forehead level so that your paddle pulls as vertically as possible alongside your kayak. You should also be sitting upright and leaning slightly forward at the hips. This position promotes torso rotation and harnesses the power of your legs for the stroke.

Week 6 **Day 3**

Name of Workout:	**JUNK PADDLE**	
Type:	Recovery	
Intensity Level:	Easy, Zone 1	
Duration:	Warm-up	10 min with some back paddling
	Workout	Beginner—65 min
		Intermediate—75 min
		Advanced—85 min
	Cool-down	10 min

INSTRUCTIONS:

Consider this workout as a true junk paddle: no focus, no drills, no technique. Just get out and paddle! Have fun. Add some edging, turning and back paddling into this session to make it more productive if you like, but be sure to keep it light.

Week 6 **Day 4**

Name of Workout:	**LSD TRIP**	
Type:	Long, slow, distance	
Intensity Level:	Easy, Zone 1	
Duration:	Warm-up	10 min, with sweeps and draw strokes in each direction
	Workout	Beginner—100 min
		Intermediate—120 min
		Advanced—140 min
	Cool-down	10 min

INSTRUCTIONS:

It is vital that you get out and put in the hours in your kayak for these long slow distance workouts, maintaining a Zone 1 heart rate the whole time. It may seem too easy, but this workout is essential to developing overall fitness and stamina. If you need to vary the theme, bringing along some friends, a picnic, some fishing rods, but be careful not to go too easy—it's still a workout.

The sun's glare off the water can be blinding—especially early or late in the day when the sun is low. Sunglasses are a great idea, although you'll want to use some type of retainer strap to make sure you don't lose them in the water. Water-specific retainers are best because they'll keep your glasses afloat if they fall in.

WEEK 1	DAY 1	DAY 2	DAY 3	DAY 4
Name of Workout	Vertical Paddle	Sprints	Junk Paddle	LSD Trip
Intensity Level	Easy and intense Zone 1 and 3 or 4	Easy and intense Zone 1 and 4 or 5	Easy Zone 1 and 2	Easy Zone 1
Duration	Beginner: 70 min Intermediate: 70 min Advanced: 90 min	Beginner: 3200 yards or meters Intermediate: 4000 yards or meters Advanced: 4800 yards or meters	Beginner: 95 min Intermediate: 105 min Advanced: 115 min	Beginner: 120 min Intermediate: 140 min Advanced: 160 min

Week 7 **Day 1**

Name of Workout:	**VERTICAL PADDLE**	
Type:	Skills and Rhythm	
Intensity Level:	Easy, Zone 1 alternating with hard, Zone 3 or 4	
Duration:	Warm-up	10 min, with some back paddling
	Workout	Beginner—50 min
		Intermediate—50 min
		Advanced—70 min
	All levels—10 min hard, 10 min easy with 2 minutes of drill	
	Cool-down	10 min

INSTRUCTIONS:

Intensity paddling and technique practice is the name of today's game. Alternate 10 minutes hard with 10 minutes easy including 2 minutes of doing the Vertical Paddle drill. When you go hard, work at a race pace or at a low Zone 4 intensity.

VERTICAL PADDLE DRILL

This drill involves paddling with your paddle shaft held as vertically as possible. A vertical paddle that pulls alongside the kayak optimizes the forward drive that you get from your stroke, while minimizing any turning effect it has.

Week 7 **Day 2**

Name of Workout:	SPRINTS	
Type:	Intervals	
Intensity Level:	Easy, Zone 1 with hard, Zone 4 or 5	
Duration:	Warm-up	20 min—add some speed pick-ups to the warm-up so that your body is ready to go fast during the workout
	Workout	200 yards or meters extreme intensity, Zone 4 or 5, followed by complete recovery in Zone 1
		Beginner—3 extreme intensity intervals
		Intermediate—4–5 extreme intensity intervals
		Advanced—4–5 extreme intensity intervals
	Cool-down	10 min

INSTRUCTIONS:

Today we introduce speed and short interval workouts. You're going to warm-up for a little longer today because you want to be thoroughly limber before you attempt these sprints.

Focus on pushing to your absolute maximum. You will work as hard as you can for a short period of time, engaging your anaerobic system. Your heart rate should be nearing Zone 5, which means you will be breathing very heavily and it should be very difficult, if not impossible to talk. This kind of workout can leave you feeling tired but elated.

All fitness levels should strive for perfect technique during these intervals even when fatigued. If you can pull together technique under duress, you will find that on easy paddles you will paddle like a pro.

One of the ultimate goals in virtually any sport is to develop perfect technique, and then learn to apply all of one's power without letting your perfect technique suffer. This is a never-ending pursuit for the highest level athletes.

Week 7 **Day 3**

Name of Workout:	**JUNK PADDLE**	
Type:	Recovery	
Intensity Level:	Easy, Zone 1	
Duration:	Warm-up	10 min, with sweeps and draw strokes in each direction
	Workout	Beginner—75 min
		Intermediate—85 min
		Advanced—95 min
	Cool-down	10 min

INSTRUCTIONS:

It's still just a junk paddle, but again, we're adding a little more time and distance to these relaxed workouts. Focus on recovery and as always, enjoy yourself out on the water. Include three 1-minute sets of easy back paddling to make the workout complete.

By this point in the program, you've probably discovered the features you like and dislike about the equipment that you're using. It's worth taking a few minutes to jot down these thoughts as you have them. It will make your next equipment purchase that much easier.

Week 7 **Day 4**

Name of Workout:	LSD TRIP	
Type:	Long slow distance	
Intensity Level:	Easy, Zone 1	
Duration:	Warm-up	10 min, with some back paddling
	Workout	Beginner—100 min
		Intermediate—120 min
		Advanced—140 min
	Cool-down	10 min

INSTRUCTIONS:

You're seeing a pattern here now aren't you? It's time for the long slow distance again which helps your body integrate all the benefits of this week's workouts. The key is economy of effort. Stay relaxed in the boat, paddle efficiently and keep drinking fluids.

ADVANCED TIP

If you're feeling energetic today, try adding a little resistance to your boat by wrapping some bungee cords around your boat to create drag in the water, or by dragging a small rope with a ball attached. You might get some confused looks from other paddlers, but the extra resistance is great for overall conditioning and fat burning.

Week 8: **Overview**

WEEK 1	DAY 1	DAY 2	DAY 3	DAY 4
Name of Workout	Breathing Rhythm	Loving the Lactic	Junk Paddle	LSD Trip
Intensity Level	Easy and intense Zone 1 and 3 or 4	Easy and intense Zone 1 and 4 or 5	Easy Zone 1 and 2	Easy Zone 1
Duration	Beginner: 80 min Intermediate: 92 min Advanced: 104 min	Beginner: 3200 yards or meters Intermediate: 4000 yards or meters Advanced: 4800 yards or meters	Beginner: 95 min Intermediate: 105 min Advanced: 115 min	Beginner: 120 min Intermediate: 140 min Advanced: 160 min

Week 8 **Day 1**

Name of Workout:	**BREATHING RHYTHM**	
Type:	Skills and Rhythm	
Intensity Level:	Easy, Zone 1 alternating with hard, Zone 3 or 4	
Duration:	Warm-up	10 min, with sweeps and draw strokes in each direction
	Workout	Beginner—60 min
		Intermediate—72 min
		Advanced—84 min
	All levels—6 min hard, 6 min easy with 1 min back paddling	
	Cool-down	10 min

INSTRUCTIONS:

While doing this 6 minutes on (hard), 6 minutes off (easy) routine, focus on timing your breaths between your strokes. During the 6 minutes of easy paddling, take one of those minutes to work on your back paddling, but keep focused on your breathing. This workout can feel more meditative and help develop greater body awareness, as well as helping to make your paddling more efficient.

When both blades are out of the water between strokes, consciously take a breath as you wind up for your next catch. If you learn to time your breathing properly, you will paddle more efficiently.

Week 8 **Day 2**

Name of Workout:	**LOVING THE LACTIC**	
Type:	Intervals	
Intensity Level:	Easy, Zone 1 with hard, Zone 4 or 5	
Duration:	Warm-up	20 min with short bursts of faster pace in the second half of the warm-up—get the body to work hard
	Workout	Beginner— 4 sets: 30 seconds hard (Zone 4 or 5), 30 seconds easy (Zone 1) 3 min Zone 1 paddling before moving to: 4 sets: 60 seconds hard, 60 seconds easy 3 min Zone 1 paddling before moving to: 4 sets: 60 seconds hard, 60 seconds easy 3 min Zone 1 paddling before moving to: 4 sets: 30 seconds hard, 30 seconds easy
		Intermediate— 5 sets: 30 seconds hard (Zone 4 or 5), 30 seconds easy (Zone 1) 3 min Zone 1 paddling before moving to: 5 sets: 60 seconds hard, 60 seconds easy 3 min Zone 1 paddling before moving to: 5 sets: 60 seconds hard, 60 seconds easy 3 min Zone 1 paddling before moving to: 5 sets: 30 seconds hard, 30 seconds easy
		Advanced— 6 sets: 30 seconds hard (Zone 4 or 5), 30 seconds easy (Zone 1) 3 min Zone 1 paddling before moving to: 6 sets: 60 seconds hard, 60 seconds easy 3 min Zone 1 paddling before moving to: 6 sets: 60 seconds hard, 60 seconds easy 3 min Zone 1 paddling before moving to: 6 sets: 30 seconds hard, 30 seconds easy
	Cool-down	10 min or longer to help clear out any feelings of "heaviness" in the body

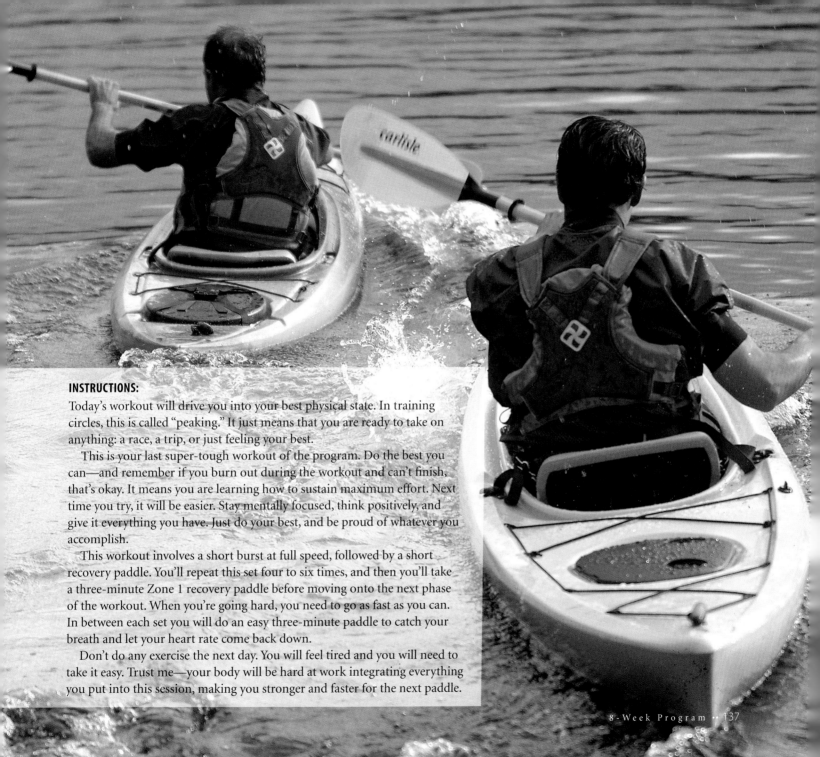

INSTRUCTIONS:

Today's workout will drive you into your best physical state. In training circles, this is called "peaking." It just means that you are ready to take on anything: a race, a trip, or just feeling your best.

This is your last super-tough workout of the program. Do the best you can—and remember if you burn out during the workout and can't finish, that's okay. It means you are learning how to sustain maximum effort. Next time you try, it will be easier. Stay mentally focused, think positively, and give it everything you have. Just do your best, and be proud of whatever you accomplish.

This workout involves a short burst at full speed, followed by a short recovery paddle. You'll repeat this set four to six times, and then you'll take a three-minute Zone 1 recovery paddle before moving onto the next phase of the workout. When you're going hard, you need to go as fast as you can. In between each set you will do an easy three-minute paddle to catch your breath and let your heart rate come back down.

Don't do any exercise the next day. You will feel tired and you will need to take it easy. Trust me—your body will be hard at work integrating everything you put into this session, making you stronger and faster for the next paddle.

Week 8 **Day 3**

Name of Workout:	**JUNK PADDLE**	
Type:	Recovery	
Intensity Level:	Easy, Zone 1	
Duration:	Warm-up	10 min, with sweeps and draw strokes in each direction
	Workout	Beginner—75 min
		Intermediate—85 min
		Advanced—95 min
	Cool-down	10 min

INSTRUCTIONS:

This is exactly the same workout as last week. Just focus on recovery and having a good time. You will probably feel stiff from the lactic sprint workout that you did two days ago, so just go out and enjoy some time on the water. This gentle paddle will help to clear any remaining lactic acid from your muscles and leave you feeling much better at the end.

Week 8 **Day 4**

Name of Workout:	**LSD TRIP**	
Type:	Long, slow, distance	
Intensity Level:	Easy, Zone 1	
Duration:	Warm-up	10 min
	Workout	Beginner—100 min
		Intermediate—120 min
		Advanced—140 min
	Cool-down	10 min

INSTRUCTIONS:

For this last long workout of the 8-week program, I recommend that you head out onto water that you have not previously paddled. Go explore an interesting area where you can practice all of the skills you have learned during the last two months. You should be feeling fit, in control and full of energy. Congratulations for making it this far. You're looking great!

CHAPTER 7:

Training Off the Water

> Complementary Sports for Endurance Development

> Strength and Power Development

Sometimes you won't be able to get on the water due to environmental or seasonal factors. Training time spent off the water is perfect for recovering from a hard kayaking workout, and is also great for improving your skills, strength and conditioning. Off-the-water conditioning can be achieved through sports like running, cycling, or (if you live near snow), cross-country skiing and snowshoeing. I find that using other sports to complement my paddling training gives me better balance in my physical development and keeps me fresh and excited about getting into my boat.

Complementary Sports for Endurance

RUNNING

Running is often the easiest off-the-water exercise to do because it requires little preparation time, can be done almost anywhere, and needs no special facilities, only a good pair of properly-fitted shoes to cushion your joints from the pounding. There are two basic types of running training: cross-country, which is done on ascending or undulating terrain, and road or track, which is done on flat or gentle terrain.

I recommend cross-country running because the trails available offer better scenery and more variety of terrain. Running hills is a great way to work your anaerobic (high intensity) system. Uphill running training is very hard so I only recommend these types of workouts to very fit or experienced runners.

Running on an athletic track is an ideal choice for determining how long it takes you to do specific distances, but running along a flat path is also beneficial for steady state training or aerobic intervals.

CYCLING

Cycling is very good for developing endurance and is an excellent alternative for anyone who either doesn't like running or is suffering from joint injuries. Indoor bike trainers or spinning bikes are good because you can adjust the resistance on them easily. Bike workouts should be varied between long distance, fartleks, steady-state aerobic, and anaerobic intervals throughout the training week. Because cycling is low-impact, it can also be a good warm-up activity.

SWIMMING

Swimming will help develop your breathing, circulatory system and upper body strength. Freestyle (front crawl) technique is the best to use as a complement to paddling. If you want to add resistance (and intensity) to your workout, try wearing really baggy swimming shorts or wear a t-shirt while you swim. You can also use controlled breathing exercises to develop your body's capacity to use oxygen effectively. Try breathing once every three to six strokes, or swimming as far as possible on one breath. Vary your training each week between steady aerobic and interval-intensive anaerobic workouts. Remember too that when weather permits, going for a swim after paddling is a great way to cool down after a hard workout.

INDOOR PADDLING

Indoor paddling is an option if you are lucky enough to live near a paddling club with paddling tanks. These are really beneficial if it is impossible to get out on the water. As an alternative, local gyms may have kayak-specific ergometers, or "ergs"—or at least a rowing-specific erg. I use a kayaking erg regularly throughout the off-season and have found it to be really beneficial in preparing for the spring. "Erging" does require a tolerance for monotony so I try to limit the time spent on these machines to an hour at a time. I use very similar workouts to what I have described in this book for on-water sessions, but focus more on long duration or aerobic intervals.

CROSS-COUNTRY SKIING

Cross-country skiing is a terrific winter sport for all-around strength and conditioning. Because I live in a place that has a distinct winter season, this is the activity I spend the most time doing while the snow is on the ground and I heartily recommend it to you as one of the best complements to

kayaking. You'll not only get excellent endurance development and burn many calories, but cross-country skiing also uses many of the same motions and muscle groups as paddling. Specifically, it works your arms, shoulders and leg muscles with little or no impact on your joints.

Cross-country skiing is the closest simulation to a true paddle stroke. Because you can choose anything from a leisurely classic ski through the woods to high-speed skate-skiing intervals, you can match the level of skiing intensity to the level of paddling intensity that you are ready for. A touring paddler can go out for a one or two hour ski across flat terrain, while those seeking a higher intensity workout can choose a trail with numerous climbs and descents.

INDOOR ROCK CLIMBING

Indoor rock climbing requires balance, coordination and upper body strength—but it's also a lot of fun and truly accessible to all levels of athletes. I have started using indoor rock climbing as a way to develop strength in the upper body, specifically for increasing forearm and grip strength. If you've never done it before, give it a try—sign up for some lessons at the local climbing gym. You can go with friends or take the family, and everyone can climb at the level appropriate for their abilities. It feels so much like playing that you might not even notice that you're getting a workout!

Strength and Power Development

Strength is generally defined as the ability to exert force against a resistance. Muscular endurance is important, but so is power if you want to maintain speed over any distance without muscle fatigue. The main goal of strength training is therefore to develop power in the muscles that you use paddling so that you can perform better. In addition, this kind of training can help to prevent injury by building healthier and stronger muscles and bones. I recommend that you consult a professional trainer at your gym for setting up a workout schedule that suits your needs.

If you live in an area that has a cold winter where you will not be able to get on the water, strength training at a gym can be a very beneficial off-season activity. Done properly, you will greatly reduce the aches and pains that are usually associated with the first few paddles in the spring and you will perform better year after year. If you live in a climate where you can paddle year-round, choose any time that feels right for you.

Be sure to focus on core strength and stability training. The core muscles are composed of the abdominal muscles, the lumbar region or lower back, and the thoracic and cervical regions of the spine (middle and upper areas, respectively). The core muscles work to stabilize the spine and provide a solid foundation for the optimal movement and function of the rest of the connected muscle groups. A strong tight core allows power generated in one part of the body to be effectively transferred to another. Core strength is essential to any sport, especially paddling, because getting power from proper rotation demands that you have a strong, stable core—although you will also develop stronger core muscles by using torso rotation when you paddle.

Any strength training you undertake should be progressive in both the intensity and duration, and should be varied to ensure proper adaptation will occur in your body.

CHAPTER 8:

Beyond the 8 Weeks

> Continuing Your Training

> Other Kayaking Activities

> Competitive Kayaking Activities

Now that you are a more fit kayaker, here are some fun suggestions as to how you might put your new, stronger body to work.

Continuing Your Training

Hopefully you don't feel like it's time to stop training just because you completed the 8-week program. My hope is that now that once you get the feel for what a training schedule looks like, you will continue on this path, customizing the program to suit your needs and ambitions—whether you just want to stay generally fit or if you are working toward a competition. Mix and match from the workouts I have provided and introduce more cross-training in the winter.

Of course, fitness requires maintenance. Let it be a lifestyle that you have chosen, one that puts your health, well-being—and fun—front and center in your priorities.

If you are customizing a training schedule for yourself, use the basic weekly pattern of the program, which essentially consists of:

- **one or two interval and skill workouts**
- **one recovery workout**
- **one long, slow distance workout**

> **If you're interested in trying whitewater kayaking, I strongly recommend that you take professional instruction so that you learn about the correct techniques and safety at the beginning.**

Other Kayaking Activities

If you're not interested in competing, but want to develop your paddling skills or take them in a new direction, consider the following kayaking activities.

WHITEWATER KAYAKING

Whitewater kayaking is very fun and is a surprisingly safe outdoor adventure sport. Like downhill skiing or mountain biking, it can be as mellow and relaxed or as adrenaline-charged as you want it to be. The sport has boomed in popularity over the last decade in large part thanks to new boat designs that have made learning easier and opened up the world of playboating. It's now as common for a kayaker to head to the river to surf their local wave for a few hours after work as it is for someone to run a section of rapids.

TOURING OR SEA KAYAKING

Using a sea or touring kayak is a great way to discover the open waters of lakes and oceans. Sea kayaking is best suited for traveling through waterways that offer little or no need to portage your gear. Storage compartments in the bow and stern are accessed through waterproof hatches. There is a surprising amount of space in these compartments: luxurious multi-day (or even multi-week) trips are possible.

With your new paddling fitness, you should have the confidence to take on bigger water and longer trips, although I recommend that you prepare yourself by reading or taking a course before doing a multi-day trip—especially to learn more advanced safety techniques. Sea kayaking is a popular sport around the world with equipment rentals and guided trips available in some very beautiful places.

Modern sea kayaks come in a variety of materials, designs and sizes to suit different paddlers and intended uses. Most sea kayaks are between 12 and 24 feet in length.

Sea kayaking can get you to some of the most spectacular places on the planet. PHOTO BY PAUL VILLECOURT

Competitive Kayaking Activities

If you're competitive and want to get involved in some racing, there are a few options to consider.

In the world of flat water paddling, you can try sprint racing and marathon racing. Spring racing takes place on calm water over relatively short and straight courses, with every competitor having their own lane. Common distances are 200, 500 and 1000 yards or meters. Because of the short course length, sprint racing is great for spectators and has been a part of the Olympics since 1936. Sprint boats are designed for one thing—to go as fast as possible, and so they are extremely narrow and light.

Marathon races are long distance races on rivers and lakes. The courses go from point A to point B and require navigating around the natural obstacles, like rocks, shallows, weeds and portages. Races start at 4 miles (or about 6 km) in length, but World Cup and World Championship races are normally about 20–25 miles (or about 35–40 km) long and involve at least two portages. Long races can be divided into several parts or stages and can last over several days. The longest marathon race in the world is the Yukon River Quest, which follows 461 miles (742 km) of the Yukon River from Whitehorse to Dawson City in Canada's Yukon Territory and is a multi-day event.

For whitewater paddling, you can try slalom and downriver races. Slalom paddlers are required to make their way down a designated section of whitewater as fast as possible while negotiating a series of hung gates. Missing a gate or touching a pole adds penalty time to your run. This is the only form of whitewater kayaking currently in the Olympics.

Downriver racing combines the speed of flat water racing with the technical aspects of whitewater paddling. The fastest time from point A to point B wins. A typical downriver course will take place on a river with continuous rapids and will cover between 500 yards or meters to 6 miles (about 10 km).

Slalom racing involves navigating through gates over a short whitewater section of river. Slalom is the only form of whitewater kayaking currently in the Olympics.

Sprint races take place on calm, straight courses, with every competitor having their own lane.

TRAINING FOR AN EVENT

If you decide to compete, here are some tips to get you ready to perform at your best.

The training period before an event is called the predatory phase. In this phase, you work towards your maximum performance so you go into the event with your greatest potential. Of course, you must plan well in advance for any races or events that you would like to undertake seriously. A good rule of thumb is to start planning eight to thirteen weeks before your main event. The longer you have to prepare the better. Also of great importance is the type of event and the distance. Prepping for a marathon race is completely different than getting ready for a sprint series. The clients I help prepare for sprint races will do plenty of speed drills and technique workouts, while for marathon paddlers, I will keep the focus on combining power and speed with extreme distance workouts.

My advice is to complete the 8-week program well in advance of your event and then move on to about a four-week event-specific preparation phase. This phase of training should be designed to suit the type and duration of the race.

The final training phase before your race is called tapering. Tapering is critical to achieving your top performance because it limits damage to muscles and lets your body recover from a lengthy training schedule. Tapering lasts approximately one week, which allows your body to adapt and recover from all of your hard work—and to give your brain time to recover as well. After all, you need to still feel excited about getting back in the boat for the race! The tapering period involves fewer and shorter workouts, but you'll maintain speed and intensity so that your muscles can recover without losing the power you've built up with training.

AWARD WINNING OUTDOORS BOOKS AND DVD'S

RECREATIONAL KAYAKING

1 Hr, DVD, $19.95

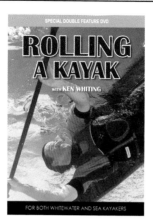

ROLLING A KAYAK

1.5 Hr, DVD, $26.95

CAMP COOKING

224 pages, Full Color, $19.95

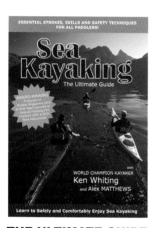

**THE ULTIMATE GUIDE
TO SEA KAYAKING**

2 Hrs, DVD, $29.95

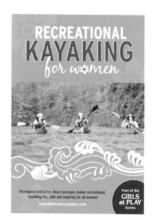

**RECREATIONAL KAYAKING
FOR WOMEN**

1 Hr, DVD, $24.95

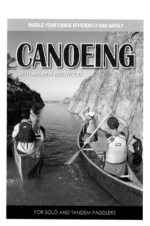

CANOEING

1.5 Hrs, DVD, $19.95

THE **HELICONIA PRESS**